ENGAGEMENT ORGANIZING

I0967911

ENGAGEMENT ORGANIZING

ENGAGEMENT ORGANIZING

The Old Art and New Science of Winning Campaigns

Matt Price

With a foreword by Allan R. Gregg

a UBC Press imprint
Vancouver . Toronto

© On Point Press, an imprint of UBC Press, 2017

All rights reserved. No part of this publication may be reproduced, stored in a retrieval system, or transmitted, in any form or by any means, without prior written permission of the publisher, or, in Canada, in the case of photocopying or other reprographic copying, a licence from Access Copyright, www.accesscopyright.ca.

26 25 24 23 22 21 20 19 18 17   5 4 3 2 1

Printed on FSC-certified ancient-forest-free paper (100% post-consumer recycled) that is processed chlorine- and acid-free.

ISBN 9780774890168 (pbk)
ISBN 9780774890175 (epdf)
ISBN 9780774890182 (epub)
ISBN 9780774890199 (mobi)

Cataloguing-in-Publication data is available from Library and Archives Canada.

Canada

UBC Press gratefully acknowledges the financial support for our publishing program of the Government of Canada (through the Canada Book Fund), the Canada Council for the Arts, and the British Columbia Arts Council.

Printed and bound in Canada by Friesens
Set in Myriad and Minion by Artegraphica Design Co. Ltd.
Copy editor: Dallas Harrison
Indexer: Lillian Ashworth

UBC Press
The University of British Columbia
2029 West Mall
Vancouver, BC V6T 1Z2
www.ubcpress.ca

This book is dedicated to organizers everywhere
who seek not the limelight but a better world.

Contents

Foreword

I first came across Matt Price in 2012 when a colleague forwarded a paper that he had written, titled "Revenge of the Beaver," and delivered at the Stonehouse Standing Circle Annual Summit earlier in the year. My colleague also informed me that the paper had caused something of a sensation and was now considered required reading among members of the progressive NGO community. In it – as he does here – Price wrote about a new way of engaging and organizing volunteer citizens that was effecting real, on-the-ground change.

After reading the article, I was surprised that Price wasn't writing about some sci-fi approach to engagement but was actually advocating for something that had always been – but seemingly had been lost and forgotten – the historical centrepiece of activism: namely, encouraging individuals to exercise control over their lives, and where they live, by empowering them to make decisions on their own and then taking responsibility for their execution. Far from being futuristic, this involved techniques such as door knocking, house meeting, petition circulating, and good, old-fashioned protesting.

What made this all different – and relevant – was that Price was providing some compelling theoretical context about why this approach is particularly appropriate and effective in the twenty-first century. He wrote about "distributed leadership," in which an organizer's role was not simply to recruit more and more volunteers to a cause but also to identify, teach, and motivate "organic" leaders and then move on, creating a "snowflake model" of networked interactions among volunteers rather than a traditional, hierarchical, command-and-control structure. The other obvious difference was that the pioneers of engagement organizing, such as Saul Alinsky and Cesar Chavez, didn't have the Internet or other digital tools that would allow them to scale their organizations rapidly and, even more importantly, allow volunteers to interact with, energize, and learn from one another – making hierarchical, command-and-control structures unnecessary.

On many levels, I was intrigued.

In the dozens of political campaigns that I was involved with in the 1980s and early 1990s, the universally accepted operating principle was that elections were won or lost based upon the "air war" – using paid advertising and the earned media generated through the leader's tour, speeches, and press conferences – and that a "ground game" – involving canvassing, making candidate brochures, and identifying local voters – was something to keep volunteers preoccupied but otherwise of little consequence.

Against this experience, however, I had noted Barack Obama's remarkable and sophisticated 2008 campaign, which had attracted over 1.5 million volunteers (and, as Price reminds us here, had been preceded and inspired by Howard Dean's run for the 2004 Democratic nomination) who had used digital tools to drive local data into central servers and allocate resources according to algorithmic-calculated opportunity. In 2012, while Senate and House Democrats were being defeated, Obama was re-elected using the same techniques but this time supported by 2.2 million volunteers.

I had also become aware of new grassroots organizations such as the Dogwood Initiative, Leadnow, and Open Media (all of which, and many more, Price writes about here), recruiting and signing up literally hundreds of thousands of activists defying authority and the status quo – rallying to ban oil tankers from the Strait of Juan de Fuca, signing petitions to challenge mandatory minimum sentencing legislation, and lobbying to maintain an open and neutral Internet.

Price's writing and these mounting examples also got me thinking about other non-political research, which caused me to question some of my earlier assumptions about behavioural change. Surveys that I had conducted on philanthropy, for example, demonstrated that the best predictors of charitable giving were not attitudes – sentiments such as "we have a responsibility to help those less fortunate than us" and "we are all each other's keepers" – but things such as attending church, making donations a part of a monthly budget, volunteering, or making payroll deductions for charity. This suggested that charitable giving was not a function of being charity *minded* so much as a structured act in which a certain kind of *behaviour* begat behaviour – in other words, the more charity was embedded in an individual's life, the more frequently she or he gave and in greater amounts. What made this conclusion surprising is that it turned normal persuasion theory on its head: it suggested that changed attitudes do not necessarily lead to changed behaviour; instead, changed behaviour will lead to changed attitudes. If you get someone to *believe* something, that person will not necessarily *do* anything; however, if you get someone to *do* something, you will likely also get that person to *believe even more strongly in what he or she is doing.*

And this is precisely what Price writes about when he introduces the reader to the "iron rule" of engagement organizing: *"never do for others what they can do for themselves."* Volunteers are empowered and given responsibility to execute their own plans because it develops their own sense of agency. By *doing* something (instead of merely being *told* to believe in something), their attitudes – their loyalty and commitment to the cause – will intensify and expand. Price makes the point concretely and simply when he quotes Jamie Biggar from Leadnow: "It's amazing how a not very political person will go from signing a petition to hosting a rally. It's because we ask."

So I began a correspondence with Price, and we met and discussed this phenomenon in more detail. And I learned from him that citizen engagement was evolving in response not only to growing frustration among activists with the responsiveness and representativeness of our leaders but also to changes in how citizens desire to be engaged and take more control over their lives.

When I was actively involved in politics, we practised what might be called citizen engagement 1.0. All communication was one way (relayed through media and news) and emanated from the inside out – you spoke, and the intended audience listened. The goal was to make people behave in a certain way (e.g., vote for your side) by telling them something credible, relevant, and salient. Again, this approach was based upon traditional persuasion theory – change attitudes and you will change behaviour. Engagement

1.0 worked well as long as the electorate was passive, trusting, and deferential to traditional authority. As Canadians shifted from deference to defiance in the late 1980s and 1990s, and as we witnessed a wholesale erosion of favourability of and trust in politicians, this inside-out messaging lost its effectiveness because hardly anyone believed the messenger – let alone the message – anymore.

It soon became apparent, however, that this loss of trust was not limited to politicians but extended to all traditional authorities, including the media. Picking up on this, elites then pivoted to citizen engagement 2.0. This newer model recognized the less deferential – and thus less hierarchical – relationship between citizen and authority and therefore offered more of a dialogue and an opportunity for the citizen's voice to be part of public discourse. Engagement 2.0 then featured things such as town hall meetings, citizen assemblies, and media series such as "It's Your Turn" that featured everyday citizens offering their solutions to problems in the community and society. Although all of this "consulting and listening" recognized the frustration of citizens, engagement 2.0 was likely doomed to failure.

Like that old saying "What's the worst part of asking for advice? Listening to it," inviting uncoordinated citizen advice largely led to nothing more than incoherence, for it was impossible to quantify or even aggregate this input. It also raised expectations that led to even more public alienation from authorities who asked for citizen advice but had no intention of acting on it.

Then came September 11, 2001. In the next seven years, North Americans' outlook changed in a way that hadn't been witnessed before. In our polling, we noted the largest number of Canadians ever saying that they were better off than they had been ten years earlier and the smallest number ever anticipating a recession in the "next year," yet levels of optimism were stuck at post-9/11 levels. Neither new concern about personal safety nor "joyless prosperity" did anything to repair the broken bond between citizens and their leaders, but it did seem to put a temporary halt to the two-decade-long erosion of trust.

But the financial meltdown of 2008–9 took the public finger off this pause button, and mistrust of "elites" started to take on a whole new form. Following citizen uprisings such as the Arab Spring and Occupy Wall Street, by 2011 *Time* named "the protester" as its "person of the year." At the same time, Price was writing "Revenge of the Beaver" and noting a quantitative and qualitative difference in the level and nature of activism around the world. Since then, we have witnessed the almost spontaneous emergence of other activist movements, such as Idle No More, Black Lives Matter, and, most recently, the Women's March on Washington. Price gives context and understanding to these developments and introduces readers to many lesser-known groups organizing citizens to take control of their lives by practising this new, digitally powered form of citizen engagement 3.0.

There are still many current examples of messaging that triumphs over organization (as Price acknowledges). When one side of a contest has an overarching message that taps into the raw nerve of public opinion more viscerally than its opponent's message, what happens in a local area or on the ground matters little (just ask Hillary Clinton, who faced the anger and desire to "Make America Great Again," or the dozen well-regarded, urban, NDP incumbents who went down to wholesale defeat in the wake of the Justin Trudeau juggernaut in 2015). But even in these cases, it still strikes me as undeniable that something new and different is happening in the fundamental relationship between citizens and leaders.

In the introduction, Price claims that "this book is primarily intended for campaign practitioners, amateur or professional." After reading it, I think that he is being far too modest. As he quotes Nicole Carty of SumOfUs, "the more we can create structures where regular people can plug in, connect to each other, stand up for what matters, the more possible it will be to transform the deepest injustices in our society." This is the subject that Matt Price explores in *Engagement Organizing*, and anyone who cares about justice, equality, and democracy will find much to learn in the pages that follow that will be inspiring.

Allan R. Gregg
Opinion researcher and a principal with
the Earnscliffe Strategy Group

Acknowledgments

I acknowledge the Cowichan Tribes First Nation, in whose traditional territory I live and where this book was written. Thank you to Randy Schmidt, Holly Keller, and the team at UBC Press for believing in this project and helping to take it to completion. I also acknowledge Jon Stahl, with whom I wrote the original engagement organizing paper that served as the inspiration for this book. Jon also gave extensive feedback on book ideas and draft language over beer and via email. I received helpful feedback from several friends and from two anonymous reviewers assigned by the publisher. All errors remain my own. I thank everyone who took the time for an interview, both those who are named in the book and those who want to remain anonymous. Thank you to Tzeporah Berman, Jen Lash, and Ivan Thompson for supporting my work over the years by helping to study the type of activity found in these pages.

I'm indebted to my parents and sisters for supporting me throughout life and providing a solid foundation so that I was able to try untraditional and risky things such as a career working in campaigns. That's a real privilege not available to everyone and I've tried to give back through my work. Thank you to my son Oliver, ten years old at the time of writing, who helpfully suggested some titles for the book. Sorry, buddy, the publisher wouldn't go for *Dave and the Missing Socks* or *Stuart Hears a Noise*. Finally, to my partner Jill, I love you, honey, and hope in some way that my writing can make me seem more talkative.

ENGAGEMENT ORGANIZING

ENGAGEMENT ORGANIZING

Introduction: Failing Well

> While you are looking, you might as well also listen,
> linger and think about what you see.
>
> – Jane Jacobs

Everybody fails sometimes. The question is whether you fail well. A big failure of mine took place several years ago when I was working with the group Environmental Defence in Toronto. We were trying to protect Ontario's renewable energy program against attacks by groups who disliked wind power. The public was broadly onside with closing the province's coal plants and shifting to cleaner energy, but there was concern in rural areas where new wind turbines were being built. Anti-wind groups popped up, led by people making a mixture of arguments about health risks and property rights. The conservative opposition party, itself rurally based and ideologically skeptical about renewable energy, also gave voice to these concerns. The provincial election of 2011 became in part a referendum on wind energy, particularly in less urban areas.

On paper, our campaign had everything going for us. Compared with the anti-wind groups, we were relatively well funded. General opinion was on our side. Science both supported the shift to renewables and indicated that anti-wind health arguments were bogus. We had the legitimacy of both the government position and a growing renewable energy industry helping to create jobs. But when the dust settled after election day, the governing party had been reduced to minority status based upon losses in anti-wind areas. Our opponents had won. We had failed.

Campaigns are complicated things with lots of variables and with human unpredictability at the core of each one. After some months passed, I began to settle on why we had lost when we should have won, and more importantly I began to apply this lesson to the future, to fail well. I realized that while we had been in our downtown Toronto office writing reports, calling journalists, running ads, and posting on Facebook and Twitter, our opponents had been on the ground in rural communities talking to people face to face, recruiting citizens to their cause, and turning them out at key moments with decision makers. We had been talking to the public in general in a shallow way while they had been focusing on deeper engagements with specific people.

This wasn't a fresh insight, but it was a timely one. Often the conditions need to be right to learn from failure and to be moved to do things differently. I had been active in a range of advocacy causes for about fifteen years and was ready for something new. A shift was under way in how campaigns are waged and won, driven in part by innovations in US presidential races and spilling over into campaigns of all kinds in Canada and around the world. My experience doing what didn't work led me to ask what did work, and I found others also asking this question. In fact, the very act of asking the question consistently was becoming incorporated into campaigns as a permanent feature.

In 2012, Sasha Issenberg published the *Victory Lab*, a book that has helped to transform modern campaigns. It describes the trend toward campaigns not only asking what works but also applying the kinds of randomized experiments to campaign tactics that have been called "prescription drug trials for democracy."[1] Do you have a million dollars to spend on a campaign to convince people of something? You could take a tenth of that money and experiment whether leafletting gets you more converts than phone calling and then allocate the remaining resources accordingly. The questioning itself is part of the shift. It's not something that ends but gets built into all campaigns. Some of the answers, though, take us back to why I failed in Ontario and to what came next.

Academics Donald Green and Alan Gerber are leaders in the emerging field of applying randomized experiments to campaigns. They have participated in dozens of experiments with political candidates and third-party groups seeking to boost voter turnout or to influence issues. They have systematically measured the use of various tactics, such as canvassing, phone banks, leafletting, and print, radio, and TV ads. Their core conclusion is common sense at one level but quite disruptive at another. Overall, they say, "the more personal the interaction between campaign and potential voter, the more it raises the person's chances of voting."[2] They find that canvassing is more effective than phoning and phoning more effective – particularly when done by caring volunteers – than leafletting. Part of the reason that the anti-wind groups won was because they got out there face to face with citizens and we didn't. They were personal, and we weren't. Again, this isn't rocket science, but the conclusion hits harder when it's confirmed by academic testing.

This is disruptive in the campaign world because, for the past few decades, we convinced ourselves that television and newspapers were king and designed our work accordingly. My first day on my first campaign job I was trained by a colleague on how to do things, shaped by the mission of the organization and by how it had gone about that mission in the past. When you are new on a job, it's not your role to question those assumptions. I started working with advocacy groups in the mid-1990s. Although we had policy goals, the main way that we measured day-to-day success was whether we were in the newspaper, on radio, or on television. We believed that this was the best way to influence decision makers, so we spent time writing reports, staging creative events, and generally trying to convince reporters to cover our issues. We were submerged by the broadcast media era, albeit near the tail end of it.

At the time, I didn't reflect on the fact that it hadn't always been this way. The groups that I worked for shared an advocacy model that emerged only after the 1960s. Sociologist Theda Skocpol traces the emergence of this model in a trend "from membership to management."[3] Since the 1800s, there have been many large volunteer membership federations active both in local civic life and in politics at all levels of government. Citizens were directly involved in these efforts as active participants. Then the 1960s brought the civil rights movement and an explosion in new rights-based groups organized more around specific issues such as women's equality and environmentalism. The growth of direct mail and foundation fundraising allowed these new groups to headquarter in political and media centres without the need or desire for active supporter engagement beyond writing cheques. Politicians and advocates alike hired experts to shape policy, media consultants to place stories, and pollsters to tell them what people thought. Average citizens stayed home. With no organized following, self-proclaimed representatives became "bodyless heads."[4] Hundreds of organizations, including the ones that I worked for, operated based upon this model until a series of shocks began to shake it up in the 2000s.

One shock in the electoral realm was Howard Dean's improbable but groundbreaking run for the 2004 Democratic Party presidential nomination, based upon leveraging the Internet for significant engagement of supporters in person and for fundraising. This showed that a campaign could in fact recruit volunteers at a scale to help conduct more personalized contacts, as Green and Gerber recommend. In 2008, Barack Obama built upon this lesson by training and structuring a massive volunteer army to help him win. Other shocks to the model were major policy setbacks, particularly regarding climate change. The failure to pass a US climate law in 2010 solidified the perception that the NGOs involved were failing because they were not mobilizing citizens, with the instructive exception of fierce grassroots opposition by the Tea Party. In Canada, the failure of international climate talks in 2009 in Copenhagen led advocates to doubt that their advocacy model was working. At the same time, Stephen Harper's aggressive record as prime minister was shocking to many in Canada, which, in turn, motivated campaign innovation.

In sum, by the time of my failure in Ontario, circumstances were ripe for a shift in how campaigns are designed and won. The core of this shift was a return to engaging people directly with grassroots organizing. And, though that wasn't new, the changed campaign landscape forged by digital tools was. I joined my friend and colleague Jon Stahl to study a handful of organizations then starting to marry grassroots organizing with new digital tools to build power and to win campaigns. Some were calling the approach "engagement organizing," and we circulated a paper describing it. The paper struck a chord in campaign circles. The feeling that we were facing new realities that called for new approaches seemed to be widespread. At the same time, the paper just scratched the surface. Today there is more from which we can learn. Campaigns have been innovating and learning practical lessons. Digital tools have become more pervasive and powerful and have continued to push the boundaries of organizing. There has been greater sharing among practitioners of challenges and solutions. There is now a more common vocabulary.

This book is therefore a deeper dive into engagement organizing to better capture the historical context in which it is emerging to uncover its core elements and to show how it is being practised today through case studies that span NGOs, unions, and political parties. This book draws predominantly from Canadian examples to explore the roots and current practices of engagement organizing, with relevance for campaigns of all kinds in Western democracies. One thing that I have realized in researching and writing this book is that we don't tell campaign stories enough. We are so busy on the campaigns themselves that we don't take time to catalogue what goes into them so that we can learn what to do better next time.

Some divide campaigns into the elements of "message" – what's on offer and how it's communicated – and "mechanics" – the nuts and bolts of what a campaign does to win. This book is focused primarily on the latter, though the mechanics of any good organizing campaign begin with listening for the message to emerge, so it's not black and white. Issues, candidates, and how they are framed will come and go relatively frequently. Campaign best practices will evolve more slowly. It's not that there aren't better and worse ways to tackle messaging, but they would take a whole book of their own. Meanwhile, as the disturbing election of Donald Trump over better-organized Hillary Clinton demonstrated, the message can still beat the mechanics – no amount of clever campaign methods makes up for an issue or a candidate that people just aren't enthusiastic about in the face of another dominating public attention and tapping into a mood for change.

This book is primarily intended for campaign practitioners, amateur or professional, working in a variety of sectors and on a variety of issues. I hope that it will be useful not only to those new to campaigns but also to those with some experience. Indeed, in researching this book, I saw more clearly the shifts under way as the broadcast era gives way to something more participatory with digital tools and the new culture that comes along with them. Although there are distinct chapters on NGOs, unions, and electoral campaigns, it is worthwhile for practitioners in any one field to check out the work in the others because there is common DNA in all three areas and things to be learned from stepping out of one's own sector. Overall, I hope, this book will serve as a high-level guide by situating campaigns in the context of recent history and by exploring real-world examples from which to draw lessons. However, this book is not a manual of the important in-the-weeds activities such as how to organize a house meeting or how to use social media. For those activities, there are more specific resources online that stay up to date more than a book can.

Here is a definition: *engagement organizing combines community organizing practices, digital tools, data, and networked communications to engage people at scale and win campaigns.* Engagement organizing can benefit campaigns of all kinds, whether political or not, and in multiple sectors – basically anywhere that directly engaging more people would help to achieve a campaign's goal. But this isn't an easy shift for many to make. Directly involving supporters or members requires trusting them and giving up some control. Having the hundreds or thousands of conversations necessary to make this happen takes time. Applying technological and data methods to the work means learning new systems and changing organizational cultures. All of this challenges how we have always done things, a powerful inertia. In my observation, innovation in engagement organizing often comes not from existing groups but from new initiatives or from organizations facing a big enough internal crisis to require a shift. Newness comes with less baggage, and discomfort is motivating. Nevertheless, campaigns can get there with intention and perseverance, and this book can help them.

Chapter 1 distills organizing principles and practices from the tradition and case studies of community organizing. These are core building blocks of engagement organizing. There are better and worse ways to directly involve people in a campaign, to help them organize to build power. Any campaign has at least an implied theory of change, and organizing puts people at the centre of it. Organizing identifies and develops leaders to own the campaign and to carry the mission. The process of cultivating leadership is never over, and leadership training plays a key role. We will look at case studies of the Metro Vancouver Alliance and the Association of Community Organizations for Reform Now, two successful community organizing groups thriving in Canada today, and Organize BC, a leadership training group for organizers.

Chapter 2 looks at how technology and data have changed the campaign landscape. It's not enough to talk just about "digital tools." Tools are part of it, but more important for campaigns to understand is how the underlying conditions are shifting with the erosion of the broadcast era. People's relationships with information are changing, the boundaries between private and public spheres are getting weaker, and now there are new opportunities to rapidly define and reach new communities to organize. Moreover, this shift has made easier the use of data to inform organizing. The case studies of Open Media and SumOfUs show how new online groups have taken advantage of these new conditions to achieve rapid growth, and the case study of the Dogwood Initiative shows how new systems help organizing scale up.

Chapter 3 describes how campaigns that are scaling up structure themselves and communicate via networks. Engagement organizing goes through a cycle of engagement with three overlapping phases of issue (re)alignment, mobilization, and distributed organizing. As the cycle turns, there is the opportunity to add people and resources to grow. Distributing leadership requires a structure that lets teams emerge and lets organizers, leaders, and team members hold one another accountable within a shared theory of change. We will look at one such structure called the "snowflake" model. Campaigns are dealing with a hybrid media environment of older broadcast outlets that are still influential and newer networked communications that require a new logic. There is a shift from *talking at* to *talking with* supporters, and to get to scale campaigns need to learn how to let supporters themselves own and carry the message by facilitating *talking among* them. Case studies for this chapter include recent US presidential campaigns, which are laboratories for scaling, and another look at the Dogwood Initiative to see the engagement cycle in action.

Chapter 4 shifts into a sector-by-sector exploration of how engagement organizing principles and practices are being applied, in this case the NGO sector. NGOs have the fewest legal constraints on what they do and how they are structured, so it's no surprise that some of the earliest adopters of engagement organizing can be found in this sector. The passing of the broadcast era is a form of disruption forcing innovation as more nimble, digitally driven NGOs compete for relevance and support. At the same time, several forms of inertia inhibit many NGOs from moving toward engagement organizing. Attitudes toward power also affect whether NGOs embrace this shift, including views on the role of power within organizing and its relationship to leadership. Case studies of Leadnow and Ecology Ottawa explore two NGOs practising engagement organizing in Canada today.

Chapter 5 examines the relationship between engagement organizing and unions. Labour is struggling today both with member engagement and with structural change in the economy that make it harder to unionize workplaces. A challenge is the postwar legal framework that has been good for unions in many ways but has also institutionalized a culture of servicing members rather than organizing them. Unions also lag behind other sectors in their use of digital tools. But there are successes to learn from in the case studies of UNITE HERE Local 75 with regard to organizing and the BC Government and Service Employees Union with regard to technology.

Chapter 6 looks at engagement organizing and electoral campaigns. In one key way political parties are more hard-wired to respond to societal shifts, such as the passing of the broadcast era, since they receive regular and disciplined feedback in the form of votes lost or gained. Chapter 6 adds to the US presidential campaigns with examples from Europe and Canada, where parties are opening themselves up to digital tools and practices and ultimately asking the question "whose party is this anyway?" Legal structures play a role in shaping such campaigns, including voting and election finance systems. Case studies include the 2010 mayoral election in Calgary and the 2015 Canadian federal election.

In the spirit of honesty and reflection, the Conclusion explores some of the challenges for and trends in engagement organizing. Practitioners are better served with eyes wide open to barriers so that they are better prepared to overcome them. I then end with thoughts on getting started and recap the lessons drawn from the chapters. Campaigners might need to make a "stop-doing list" to create the space for a shift to engagement organizing practices.

At any given moment, there are thousands of campaigns under way in Canada and around the world to try to shape public opinion or public policy, and during elections our environment seems to be full of them. But what separates those that win from those that lose? The answer to that question is a moving target. What worked yesterday might not work tomorrow. We are entering an era when the broadcast media model that has dominated the past few decades is being eroded in a digital evolution in which direct engagement of citizens at scale is now possible, both online and offline. It is not that TV will cease to be a powerful campaign tool but that it will increasingly fit side by side with a range of tactics that engage people directly. Campaigns that win today are those that understand this trend and design themselves to capture it, to practise engagement organizing.

chapter 1

Organizing Principles and Training

If you don't like what you got why don't you change it?
If your world is all screwed up, rearrange it.

– Trooper

Twelve years ago, Marva Burnett was making dinner in her Scarborough apartment when she heard a knock on the door. A young woman was there from the Association of Community Organizations for Reform Now (ACORN), a group that organizes in low- and moderate-income communities to make positive changes for families in them.[1] She asked Burnett whether she was facing any problems and was told about the pest infestation in the rental building. The ACORN organizer said that there was a way to fix this problem by working together with others, so Burnett invited her in. Soon Burnett joined with her neighbours in an action to highlight the infestation, witnessed by local media. As a result, the city issued a work order to clean up the building. Burnett felt great and was ready for more. Today she is the elected president of ACORN Canada.

Grassroots organizing is hardly new. As organizing expert Marshall Ganz points out, Moses used organizing methods in ancient Egypt, where he created a structure in which a leader was designated for every ten people, and for every ten leaders one representative, and so on.[2] Organizing takes place wherever people believe that they can better meet their needs together than separately, and it has been used throughout history by churches, unions, NGOs, political parties, and citizens of all kinds. Community organizing is a distinct practice of organizing, with a historical focus on economic justice issues at the local level, where disadvantaged people are brought together to act on their collective self-interest. It has developed over several decades, with established methodologies based upon a good deal of trial and error.

These methodologies were laid down before the Internet and are central to the distinction between community organizing and engagement organizing. The latter is built upon the changed campaign landscape that digital tools and the use of data afford campaigns of all kinds. Some might argue that there's no real distinction because the Internet hasn't changed the fundamentals of human psychology, but there is an undeniable difference in the ability to hit larger organizing scales quickly today and in the ability to directly engage large numbers of people on issues of all kinds and across geographies. Nevertheless, community organizing has much to teach about how to bring people together to build power. As we will see, the Internet alone cannot do this with consistency or resilience, particularly in the face of entrenched interests, so organizing is needed too. This chapter explores the tradition and practices of community organizing, together with leadership training, and includes the present-day case studies of the Metro Vancouver Alliance, ACORN Canada, and Organize BC.

The Tradition and Practices of Community Organizing

Saul Alinsky is considered by many to be the godfather of community organizing. Inspired by the tactics of labour organizer John L. Lewis and the industrial unions of the 1930s, Alinsky started organizing in the Back of the Yards area of Chicago, the notoriously poor meat-packing district immortalized by author Upton Sinclair in the novel *The Jungle*. Alinsky achieved notoriety, wrote two books about his thoughts and experiences, and became the best-known advocate of community organizing. He also mentored dozens of organizers who themselves pioneered new methods and in turn mentored others. His legacy is reflected in the Industrial Areas Foundation (IAF), an organization that Alinsky founded but that scaled up only after his death in 1972. Not everything that he wrote should be considered gospel. Indeed, he himself preached pragmatism and didn't like it when organizers narrowly interpreted his writings. But in his books and experiences we begin to see the shapes of many of the practices of community organizing relevant to engagement organizing.

A key starting point is why organizers choose to do what they do. Why bring people together in the first place rather than just write a report or lobby the government? Today we've come to call this having a "theory of change," a picture of how the world works and what best to do to influence it. At its most basic level, a theory of change says that "if we do X, then Y will result." For example, a community group working on protecting a municipal program from budget cuts might have a short-term theory of change like this: "If we get 100 phone calls to each councillor before the budget vote, a majority will vote to retain the program." The stronger and more compelling the theory of change, the stronger the campaign will be. There are multiple valid theories of change, but which ones are related to the tradition of organizing and how it approaches change? Alinsky made it clear that he saw the world "as an arena of power politics moved primarily by perceived immediate self-interests,"[3] and by coming together people can build the power necessary to compete with other interests, particularly those with money. This reflected his starting point of working with people in poverty, but the basic point is building power by having people act together.

Alinsky recognized people's discomfort with the concept of power. We often say that power corrupts, but he believed that the corruption lies in us rather than in power itself.[4] He recognized that, at its most basic, power is simply the ability to act. But this can mask a distinction between "power to" and "power over," where the latter is more explicitly relational and implies a kind of coercion – making others do something that they wouldn't normally do. The distinction is more one of degree, though, given that the ability to act is almost always relational. Each situation will have different actors with different levels of alignment or opposition, and a campaign will necessarily want to get as far as possible by bringing people willingly onside before dealing with entrenched opponents. Then a more explicit element of power might be necessary to win. This can be unsettling.

Decades after Alinsky's death, this discomfort with power persists. University of Toronto professor Judith Taylor relates a battle started in 2009 to stop diesel trains from disrupting and polluting residential neighbour-hoods in Toronto along a new route. Opponents believed in the ability of truth and information to win the day, and they avoided making waves, instead using reason and ethical arguments with the government to persuade it to choose electric trains instead.[5] The citizens were surprised when the govern-ment proceeded with the diesel trains, and one concluded that "we tried logic, and morality, and all these other kinds of arguments, and none of them work[ed]. I guess we just didn't know how to go about making politicians feel they better do the right thing."[6] Taylor notes that citizens still widely expect governments to incorporate rational feedback and are shocked when that doesn't happen, leading to anger and a host of other emotions.[7]

The pervasiveness of power politics offends our sense of fairness. We have a hard time adjusting to the need to build power if we want to get things done. Even if we don't accept Alinsky's view that life is entirely about self-interest, the practice of organizing is nevertheless based upon the belief that having the best information isn't going to lead to a win. An organizing-based theory of change will always include bringing people together in suf-ficient numbers and with enough coherence to have the power to make things happen. Here power equals the quantity and depth of relationships aligned around a mission and the collective resources that those relationships can bring to bear.

Alinsky's approach involved having an organizer bring together leaders of existing institutions in a neighbourhood – churches, civic groups, unions – around a common program. Other organizers focus instead on bringing together individuals rather than institutions. A leader won't necessarily be the loudest person in the room (and probably wouldn't be), but rather some-one who can bring others along and who will put in time and effort. Alinsky advocated starting where people are at, prejudices and all, and initiating a conversation about the challenges that they face. Today you still hear organ-izers talk about starting where people are at rather than where they would like them to be. The organizing goal is to have people work together to ex-perience winning change rather than being told about it. "It is impossible to overemphasize," Alinsky wrote, "the enormous importance of people's doing things themselves."[8] The organizer's job is not to carry the flag but to identify and cultivate leaders to do so. This is a rejection of a service model in which a person is doing something on behalf of somebody else – the core idea is to help people help themselves. An organizer is therefore pushing people as skillfully as possible to develop their own agency. One organizer writes that "an axiom of organizing is that every good organizing conversation makes everyone at least a little uncomfortable. And it's a conversation that must be had."[9] There is a delicate dance of the organizer not only recruiting and developing leaders but also being accountable to them. Organizers need to be transparent about their roles in the decision-making process. As leaders step into their roles, they form a decision-making body. Some form of people's organization is thereby formed.

What to take on and how to take it on are guided by a power analysis, variously called "power mapping" or "power structure analysis," which uncovers the networks of power surrounding an issue – who are the decision makers, who are their allies and opponents, and what are the best points of leverage. A necessary part of the analysis is a methodical uncovering of the power – relationships and resources – that those seeking change can bring to bear.[10] By conducting this analysis together in a participatory way, the collective knowledge of supporters is leveraged, and the belief that they can be powerful and win is cultivated. For Alinsky, an issue that an organization tackles needs to be "specific, immediate, and realizable."[11] He was not above tricking new leaders by first having them take on and win easy issues to build confidence. The organizer's job, he said, "is to give the people the feeling that they can do something, that while they may accept the idea that organization means power, they have to experience this idea in action."[12] The tactics that an organization uses are flexible, adapting to the situation as needed. They can be as traditional as bake sales or as radical as civil disobedience. Once an issue is won, another is chosen to maintain momentum. This method is used to build power over time, instilling confidence by winning issues, drawing in more people, and taking on bigger issues.

The focus on gradually building power and winning issues is a hallmark of community organizing. But there is a debate in organizing circles about goal setting and about the time frames involved. The community organizing approach is to break bigger goals into bite-sized chunks and to keep people engaged by winning smaller things one at a time. A different movement-building approach might set more symbolic goals that are harder to realize but that inspire more people to get involved more quickly.[13] Winning in that context might involve a shift in public opinion that sets the stage for bigger policy shifts later. Others have started to advocate for "Big Organizing," which says that people are more inspired to take on bigger changes right away without the gradual cultivation of leadership.[14] Common to all organizing approaches, however, is the desire to keep people engaged over time, which requires a theory of change they believe in; if they don't think that they can achieve progress, then they'll opt out.

Although Alinsky worked out of Chicago, he mentored Fred Ross in California. Ross built a network of organizations under the banner of the Community Service Organization. His methods differed in that he focused more on organizing individuals than on organizing organizations. He developed the tactic of the house meeting while organizing farm workers. A farm crew member would host the rest of his work crew and the organizer at his or her house for a meeting, and at the end of the meeting the organizer would ask somebody to do likewise with a new circle of friends and acquaintances, thereby expanding the group.[15] Ross codified how house meetings should unfold, with chairs in a circle, a tight agenda, and stories of successful collective action. Questions would lead to discussion, and skeptics in the circle would be brought onside by enthusiasts. Recruitment would therefore take place in a trusted social setting and lead to more recruitment at the next house meeting. As Ross said, "the house meeting is such a great tool because it is the best way of doing a very, very thorough, systematic job in a blazing way. Every organizer becomes a social arsonist, able to set people on fire in a milieu that invites the best possible exchange between the organizer and those present."[16] House meetings have been used effectively in organizing campaigns everywhere.

Ross also helped to recruit a young farm worker named Cesar Chavez to be an organizer. Chavez would go on to lead one of the great organizing drives of the twentieth century, the creation of the United Farm Workers union. Ganz has written about this drive,[17] and he joined Chavez after working in the civil rights movement. Chavez faced competition from established unions with access to greater financial resources, but he prevailed with a flexible mix of community organizing practices and culturally appropriate tactics, making the drive more of a movement. He used the house meeting method and built in social benefits for members joining his union, such as a credit union and a death benefit like those in Mexican burial societies. Key meetings were held in churches, and events drew on religious symbols. Chavez also used large-scale consumer boycotts against farm products as an organizing tactic. Today unions might call this an "integrated" campaign.

After Alinsky died, his legacy was enhanced by his successors at the IAF. Ironically, it took his passing to build a larger and more successful coalition since Alinsky was not strong on managing his own organization. Edward Chambers helped to institutionalize and grow the IAF into a network of over sixty organizations, mostly in the United States but also in Canada, the United Kingdom, Australia, and Germany. Chambers also helped to develop the IAF methodology into a slower, more deliberate process of building. Rather than jumping right into action, he believed that "issues follow relationships. You don't pick targets and mobilize first; you connect people in and around their interests."[18] The foundation of this is what the IAF calls the "relational meeting," in which stories are exchanged and people's talents and energies are uncovered for the purpose of forming a relationship around which to organize. These meetings take place with leaders who already have followings. It might take months or even years of such meetings and group deliberation to build a solid and lasting foundation for action.

The IAF formalized Alinsky's dictum that organizing needs to help people develop their own agency into the "iron rule" – *never do for others what they can do for themselves.*[19] It also developed the practice of reflection following activities. Writes Chambers: "The thirty or thirty-five minutes spent in evaluation are organizationally more important than the action."[20] The IAF works on the model of organizing organizations, and in the United States it draws heavily on religious institutions. As one IAF organizer says, "most of scripture is about the relationship of the community to the poor. So, if you probe religious teachings deeply, they lead you to a democratic life."[21]

ACORN is an example of organizing individuals rather than organizations. Founded in 1970, it organizes in low-income communities by initiating a drive to identify people to form an organizing committee. That committee in turn stages a neighbourhood meeting to decide on an initial issue to tackle and to set up a democratically run chapter. In contrast to the IAF, ACORN has historically been wary of working with other groups until it has built a base of its own and wary of established community leaders who might bring a different agenda to the table than that of the membership.[22] Also, ACORN differs from the IAF not just in its organizing individuals but also in its moving to action quickly.

This account of community organizing is incomplete but intended to bring out some core concepts. As with any discipline, dogmatism can creep in regarding what is the one best way to conduct community organizing, but at its core it is pragmatic. Good organizing is as much an invitation as a proposal, and those who accept the invitation will shape the practice. Community organizing has adapted and evolved in response to the times and will continue to do so. The lessons learned from decades of trial and error endure and underpin the practice of engagement organizing outlined in this book.

Leadership Training

Leaders are the core of organizing. Without them, you cannot scale a campaign. With them, you can multiply your impact. Leadership development never ends, and training is a key part of the process. Other types of training can sometimes focus on "hard" skills such as data management or door knocking, but that's not what is meant by leadership training. Instead, it's about other skills such as inspiring and facilitating others, with the best leadership candidates being those whose personality matches those kinds of skills. Training can also be a way to bring new people more deeply into the campaign and to make a connection with its theory of change. There are various leadership training programs for organizing, albeit with similarities.

The IAF runs a ten-day training program as well as shorter multiple-day ones. Most of the content centres on its organizing principles and its broader philosophy of politics.[23] Trainees are invited to role-play a scenario that teaches them pragmatic advancement of interests rather than assertion of principles. There is also an emphasis on personal development and on getting in touch with an expansive definition of "self-interest" – not selfishness but interest in relation to others and not just material interest but also interest in expression and meaning. This serves as the basis for developing relationships around which to organize. The IAF also teaches about power, teams, stories, one-on-one meetings, house meetings, designing actions, evaluations, and more.

ACORN's training reflects its model of quickly moving to action. Participants learn about power, mounting an organizing drive, elements of a successful campaign, turning people out, and ACORN campaigns already under way at the local, regional, or national level. In a document called "Prepping Leaders," ACORN states that "the wrong way is to tell people what to do; the right way is talk through and figure out what to do together. As with any organizing task, spend most of your time asking rather than telling."[24] Preparing leaders in the ACORN model is coaching people through concrete plans of action for specific events. Leaders are training on the job.

Both the IAF and ACORN offer leadership training to their members, making it harder to access for others. Another training source more widely accessible has been developed by Ganz. After working with Chavez, he went on to become a professor at Harvard University and now teaches leadership training through the Leading Change Network.[25] He helped develop an elegant framework that shares some similarities with IAF and ACORN training. The framework has five practices: telling stories, building relationships, structuring teams, strategizing, and acting. Here is a brief outline of those practices.

Useful at the start is how the Ganz framework defines leadership and organizing: "Leadership is accepting responsibility for enabling others to achieve purpose in the face of uncertainty."[26] This is not the version of a leader out in front carrying the flag but one in which a leader is helping others to do so. Organizing is then defined as "leadership that enables people to turn the resources they have into the power they need to make the change they want."[27]

Turning to the practices, telling stories can seem flaky to a hard-bitten campaign manager, but in fact stories are how we make sense of our world, how we organize and give meaning to information. Campaigns are about making connections, and stories do this well. Ganz recommends that this kind of story be structured around three phases: a story of "self," a story of "us," and a story of "now." In other words, the story says "Here's who I am, this is what we have in common, and here's what we're going to do about it."[28] The story makes a connection at the level of shared values. Interestingly, a Tea Party group has a similar story structure, called "Me, Together, Do."[29]

Stories are used to build relationships, and this often takes place for organizers in one-on-one meetings or at small gatherings such as house parties.

An intentional structure is brought to these meetings so that they are effective, including making a specific, or "hard," request. Leaders are often structured into teams, which in turn can be structured into a "snowflake" model (see Chapter 3). Teams offer ongoing relationships, key to sustaining commitment, as well as the opportunity for shared purpose and mutual accountability, key for effectiveness. Teams have in common with army units the bonding that takes place when people undertake action together. Organizers provide coaching to team leaders to problem-solve, and team leaders in turn are encouraged to provide coaching to team members.

Leaders expect to be a part of the strategy process and to make collective decisions. For Ganz, this involves asking "who are our people?" before defining the problem and the goal. This reinforces an organizing theory of change in which direct engagement of people is central to acting. "Our people" are a community until organized, after which they are a constituency. Participants are trained to do a power analysis, both of who has power now in relation to the problem at hand and of how to generate it. Acting requires that leaders help to set tactics and timelines. The best tactics make progress toward the goal while developing other leaders and building the organization. Those given tasks need to see how they fit into the theory of change while being given autonomy to act and space for later evaluation.

The Ganz framework is flexible enough to be adapted to most campaigns serious about distributed leadership. The training program is available through the Leading Change Network and other training bodies.

Case Studies

Community organizing has a tradition going back decades, and it is practised successfully today. Various groups do this kind of work in Canada. Here I focus on two of them, the Metro Vancouver Alliance and ACORN Canada. I also explore Organize BC, which isn't a campaign but builds leadership capacity for other campaigns through training.

The Metro Vancouver Alliance: Organizing Organizations
With about a month to go before the 2014 municipal election, Vancouver's mayoral candidates were invited to an "accountability assembly" hosted by the Metro Vancouver Alliance (MVA), a broad-based alliance of community,

faith, and labour groups in the Vancouver region.[30] The candidates listened while representatives from about fifty local churches, unions, and NGOs stood up and asked for a commitment that the city would pay its staff and contractors a living wage. Not only did each candidate make that commitment, but also, when the issue later came up for a vote in council, every councillor voted for it, including the right-leaning councillors. The MVA had spent years building this influence and had harnessed it at the right moment.

The MVA is an affiliate of the IAF. In Chicago, Alinsky used the approach of bringing together existing neighbourhood entities – churches, community groups, and others – and the IAF went on to systematize this approach. Each group that joins a local affiliate pays dues, putting the initiative on a more stable financial footing. This is one of the key advantages of organizing organizations rather than individuals.

The IAF also fleshed out what it calls the approach of "relational organizing," which starts by building relationships among the leaders of a critical mass of groups before agreeing on an issue to tackle together. Contentious subjects are left at the door, and consensus is built. This takes time. A paid organizer works with leaders from the member groups to grow the local organization, build relationships, engage in deep listening, and conduct training. Once issues are selected, a variety of tactics is employed, including public meetings at which elected officials are asked to make specific commitments.

The organizer's job is to support the leaders as they pursue actions. The IAF uses one-on-one meetings to recruit and cultivate leaders. It also holds more formal leadership training sessions. Reflection and evaluation are core parts of IAF organizing, both to improve performance and to assess reactions to actions and what can be learned.[31]

Deborah Littman became the organizer for the MVA in 2011 after working with the British IAF affiliate called London Citizens, now part of Citizens UK.[32] During her first exposure to the group, she was impressed that London Citizens was pulling in an incredibly diverse group to work together – young people, Somali immigrants, and ministers. Littman returned to her native Canada and spent her first two years at the MVA bringing groups together and building relationships before any issue was chosen. Littman coaches MVA members on the practical application of power. Vancouver is known for protest marches that end up on the steps of the Vancouver Art Gallery. Littman often asks people "What has the curator of the art gallery ever done to you?" Her point is that campaign energy is often misdirected into empty action. Instead, the MVA cycle begins with research and a power analysis, moves to the campaign, and then conducts an evaluation of it. If there is to be an action, it would be directed at those who have the power to make decisions strategically related to the goal.

It wasn't until 2014 that the MVA settled on four issue areas: social inclusion, transit, poverty, and housing. At the time of writing, Littman has helped to recruit fifty-six groups into the MVA. Local conditions in Vancouver mean that labour plays a greater role in the MVA than it does in many US affiliates in places where unions are weaker. Churches are often stronger in the United States, particularly in black and Hispanic neighbourhoods, where they are a primary vehicle of engagement for people with leadership qualities. Once institutional members sign up, a governance structure is created. At an annual general meeting, the MVA elects a board composed of three directors from faith groups, three from labour groups, and three from community groups. It uses delegates' assemblies at which each member group sends two representatives to debate and ratify campaigns. It establishes committees for various roles, including core campaigns, education, and fundraising. The MVA has both a non-profit and a charitable arm to be able to fundraise from foundations. It receives 60–70 percent of its budget from dues from member groups and fundraises for the remainder. Littman is the only MVA organizer to date, and she believes that there should be another, but the budget is limited.

A story shows the value of the MVA approach. In late 2014, the 230 staff at the Inglewood Care Centre in West Vancouver discovered that they could lose their jobs when the owner moved to change the staffing subcontractor. This had happened several times already, causing uncertainty and leading to grim conditions. Littman realized that the union representing the workers and the religious institutions in the area around Inglewood were members of the MVA. She helped to mobilize the local churches to host meetings about the situation, to send representatives to meet with the health authorities, and to send a letter to the owner. The owner backed down and signed an improved agreement with the union. It came to light that the care centre was approaching city council with plans to expand the facility, which required local support and good relations with neighbours such as local churches. This gave the MVA more leverage. Littman says that this kind of collaboration would never have happened without the relational organizing that the MVA had done. It would not have occurred to the union to reach out to the churches, or to the churches to get involved in this way, even though the events were taking place right in their backyard.

People note that the IAF approach of bringing together diverse actors to listen to one another and campaign together builds the kind of "bridging social capital" that sociologists such as Robert Putnam say we have lost over the past decades, to the detriment of our politics. Rather than shouting at one another through the media, diverse groups talk instead about what they do agree on and what they can do together. Although the approach of organizing organizations can bring better financial and organizational stability, it also has its challenges. One is the nature of potential member groups themselves. For example, many unions currently suffer from low member engagement and thus might not bring a lot of energy to the table. The IAF's answer to this problem is to help member institutions revitalize themselves, but this nevertheless eats up organizational bandwidth. Another challenge is that the model of slowly building relationships and consensus can limit the ability to be nimble and visible in today's digital age, in which issue cycles move more quickly.

Nonetheless, the IAF approach has produced results in many places. IAF affiliates are large in the American Southwest and have achieved significant policy victories in states such as Texas. And in Britain Citizens UK is powerful enough that it had all three main candidates for prime minister at its election debate in 2011, and it has helped to drive a nationwide conversation about community organizing. Littman is confident that the MVA will continue to grow and that other Canadian affiliates will take shape in cities such as Edmonton, Calgary, and Victoria, where building is already under way.

ACORN Canada: Organizing Individuals

In 2003, Winnipeg native Judy Duncan was finishing up a degree at the University of British Columbia and looking for work.[33] She stumbled across a newspaper ad for a job in Seattle doing community organizing and decided to apply for it. She was invited to a two-day training course with the Washington chapter of ACORN. What Duncan didn't know at the time was that she was destined to help bring the organization to Canada.

Founded in 1970 by Wade Rathke, ACORN grew to national prominence in the United States before splintering under the weight of external attacks and internal missteps and then rebranding in 2010. Rathke got his start in Springfield, Massachusetts, working with welfare recipients to maximize their benefits, and by his own admission he knew little about organizing. By knocking on doors, he built a local organization that successfully lobbied city hall for more benefits, and he courted controversy with confrontational tactics.[34] Although Rathke was hooked on organizing for economic justice issues, he wanted to go broader and bigger, and in 1970 he moved to Arkansas to found ACORN and work on multiple issues affecting low-income communities. He built multiple chapters, eventually jumping state lines to build a national network, and later set up initiatives in other countries.

Today ACORN Canada is faithful to the methodology laid down by Rathke. The ACORN model differs from the IAF model in that its primary focus is on organizing individuals rather than organizations. With the group's focus on organizing in low-income areas, the process begins with an analysis of which places are ripe for organizing drives. Marva Burnett's Scarborough, Ontario, neighbourhood, for example, made the cut. An organizer goes door to door asking questions about the challenges that people are facing and making a pitch about tackling the challenges together with neighbours by joining ACORN. When there is a critical mass of about thirty people, an organizing committee meeting is set, with the expectation that about a third of those invited will show up.

As one ACORN organizer says of people's experience in the initial organizing committee (OC) meeting, "the first OC meeting is kind of a spiritual experience – 'I'm not alone; there are other people who feel the same way I do'; it's a magical moment of community."[35] The organizing committee plans for a bigger neighbourhood meeting, recruiting attendees and developing a proposal to tackle a common issue. The organizer gives the criteria for an issue: it should be winnable, visible, and affect more than just a few people. In researching an issue, ACORN does an analysis of power and asks a number of questions. Who controls the issue? To whom are they accountable? To whom do they listen? At the community meeting, the proposal to tackle a common issue is debated, modified, and ratified; volunteer officers are elected; and members are signed up with the collection of dues. A chapter is born.

ACORN Canada charges between fifteen and thirty dollars a month for membership dues, a practice that sometimes raises eyebrows given its work with low-income people but a practice rooted in the philosophy that people need to help themselves. "We pay dues for everything in life," says Burnett, "so why not to help yourself? It makes us better off in the long run, so it's worth it." An action follows the community meeting within several days to keep people engaged. By this time, a chapter is established with leadership by members who shape what happens next.

At the time of writing, ACORN Canada has twenty-two chapters across the country. Duncan often says that "if you aren't growing, you are dying." One way that ACORN recruits new members is by offering free income tax help during tax season and encouraging potential members to join the organization. As members achieve victories on issues important to them, such as rental apartment conditions, they are encouraged to look at the root causes of problems and to take on bigger things. "You can win stoplights from here to eternity," says Rathke, "but unless your organization addresses the question of who has the power to control what happens in a neighbourhood, a city, a county, or a state ... all your organization will achieve is a proliferation of stoplights in low to moderate neighborhoods."[36] Chapters work on local issues but also send representatives to citywide and nationwide ACORN committees to work on larger issues.

In 2013, BC ACORN leader Rachael Goodine brought to the larger group the issue that, like thousands of others in British Columbia, part of her child support payments in her disability cheques were being clawed back because the father of her child paid some support. This issue created hardship for many low-income children in British Columbia. ACORN started an "End the Clawback" campaign with a series of demonstrations at social service offices, meetings with officials, coalition building, and media work. The campaign included a Mother's Day "Poverty Potluck" to highlight the unhealthy food that disabled mothers had to eat. In the 2015 BC budget, the government ended the clawback, in effect giving about 5,000 low-income children $13 million per year.

A paid organizer might have up to five chapters to help manage. His or her job is to cultivate volunteer leaders and to stay in the background. If an organizer is quoted in the media instead of a leader, then he or she must buy all of the other organizers a beer. With this model of organizing individuals, ACORN faces challenges both in funding its work and in retaining its members. Only about 15 to 20 percent of ACORN Canada's budget comes from membership dues, and it hustles to fundraise from other sources. ACORN is also known for paying its organizers modestly.[37] In terms of keeping things together, some of ACORN's work involves reorganizing chapters that have lost people or energy.

In its ten years in Canada, ACORN has had victories small and large. It has helped to improve conditions in hundreds of apartment buildings and pioneered landlord licensing in Toronto. It has helped to achieve living wage bylaws in cities such as New Westminster. Provincially, it has helped to bring in the regulation of predatory payday lending practices in Manitoba, Ontario, and British Columbia. At the time of writing, it was engaged in working for affordable Internet for low-income Canadians.

Organize BC: Beyond the Service Model

Organize BC is a training group for organizers.[38] Coordinator Peter Gibbs distinctly remembers the story of one training participant, told as a child that because her parents were divorced she'd never succeed in life.[39] She went on to become the elected municipal representative for 8,000 people on Vancouver Island. Gibbs has helped to shape dozens of personal stories in leadership development training. He admits that he mentally checks out when people start spewing facts, especially when he already agrees with them. But stories keep him interested. Humans are wired to make sense of the world through stories, and embracing this is a cornerstone of the leadership training that Organize BC delivers.

The program draws heavily from the Ganz leadership training framework. In 2013, a few NGOs in British Columbia came together around the need to work differently to win more. They saw the success of the organizing approach of the Obama presidential campaigns and wanted to adapt it to their work. They saw joint training as one way to make that happen, particularly in the early days, when no group had enough in-house expertise. Organize BC first tapped American trainers to help develop local trainers. Gibbs sees the Ganz framework as a broad set of principles largely applicable to many contexts globally, and certainly in any Western democracy. This includes Canada, even though more effort is sometimes needed to get Canadians to make "hard" (specific) requests of others because of greater cultural politeness.

Although Organize BC started out training paid NGO organizers, it now typically trains volunteers of the participating groups. This assumes that groups sending people to train subscribe to a theory of change that embraces the notion of distributing volunteer leadership in campaigns. Gibbs says that one of the biggest challenges that trainers like him face globally is not the training sessions themselves but working with groups to implement the lessons. "The groups that have the most success, there's top-to-bottom organizational buy in," he says. Groups that aren't fully sold on distributing leadership might cherry-pick the storytelling training but don't use it to truly engage people in their missions. To address this challenge, Organize BC is starting to deliver a pre-training workshop with core decision makers of some participating groups to reach clarity on theory of change and strategy.

Sometimes groups starting out aren't sure what they need. Organize BC once worked with a new group outside Vancouver that twice postponed the training session date. Gibbs called the key person and discovered that she'd had trouble filling seats for the training. Over the phone, he coached her on the practice of recruitment: making a personal connection, making a specific request, and so on. After twenty people showed up and completed the training, she said, "Peter, you just taught the group the things you told me on the phone. That's why all these people are here. This stuff really works!"

Storytelling often gets the most attention in training but can sometimes be taught as if the trainee needs to give a speech, which doesn't happen often. Organize BC has started training people how to use the "self, us, now" storytelling framework in one-on-one meetings in what one experienced BC practitioner calls "the sweet sauce" of organizing. First, ask questions to get the meeting attendee to tell her or his story (self), tell yours and make the connection between the two (us), and wrap up with how they can plug into the campaign (now). This can also be done at house meetings. What happens after the training session is critical. Trainers know that trainees need to be plugged in immediately, that much of the learning happens with practice, and that groups therefore need a follow-up plan before training happens. One tactic is to have people fill out a postcard at the end of the training on which they write down their goals and to send it back to them a month later as a reminder. In the meantime, the organizer can read the cards and follow up with the most promising trainees with one-on-one meetings to plug them in properly.

Organize BC facilitates a community of practice for more advanced organizers. Some organizers might be isolated in a remote place or in a small organization without any help. A peer coaching network pairs up organizers who wish to touch base periodically to talk through challenges. Once or twice a year twenty to thirty senior BC organizers go on a retreat to work through more advanced challenges such as how to restructure volunteer teams without losing people. Some groups deliver all or part of the curriculum themselves in house. This can happen during campaign pushes when time is of the essence or when something more tailored fits better. The advantage of joint training is more cross-pollination of both training methods and trainees from different groups. Gibbs recounts once travelling to the BC Interior and having the local organizer tell him "just the fact that you are this guy from Victoria our people don't know makes them take the training more seriously."

Over a three-year period, Organize BC has helped to train hundreds of volunteer leaders, thereby enabling several NGOs such as Leadnow and the Dogwood Initiative to scale up their campaigns. Organize BC began with the support of a single large donor and has since started to explore more fee-for-service activities to diversify its funding base. Time will tell whether it can raise enough money this way. Like other capacity builders, Organize BC faces challenges convincing donors that it is a key part of the organizing ecosystem.

Before Gibbs was part of Organize BC, he was on a three-person canvass crew for a local NGO when he was asked to bring "his people" to a training session in a month's time. Not knowing if they had people to bring, his crew stopped canvassing and started recruiting. Twenty people showed up, and twelve joined teams. Some months later, only six remained. But by then those six had recruited about 100 people who became a consistent organizing core in the Victoria area. This is how training and scaling go together. Gibbs says that Organize BC rejects the service model in which it is doing something on behalf of somebody else rather than helping people help themselves. "My job is organizing organizers," he says. One way is by running training sessions, but it's more about helping organizers to meet their campaign needs. Organize BC is now running some training sessions where its core staff doesn't deliver any material but coach other trainers to do so. This is building capacity so that, if Organize BC disappears tomorrow, there will still be a crew of people capable of doing the work.

Lessons for Engagement Organizing

Community organizing has a rich tradition with thriving groups making gains today. It gives us tried-and-true principles for working directly with people to develop their own power. There will never be a substitute for bringing people together to develop their own agency, leadership, and solidarity. In the following chapters, I explore how erosion of the broadcast era driven by digital tools has provided new opportunities to bring people together, but I will carry forward organizing principles highlighted in this chapter for engagement organizing:

- *Develop an organizing-based theory of change about people acting collectively.* In all organizing, power is built by the quantity and depth of relationships aligned around a mission and the resources that those relationships can bring to bear.

- *Listen for common cause.* Organizing starts with questions, not answers. As Alinsky said, "you organize with your ears, not your mouth."[40] Which issues do your people have in common?

- *Cultivate and train leaders to work with others to carry the mission.* Organizers do not do things for people but with them. Identify leaders and cultivate them by giving them responsibility. Use training and mentoring to develop skills and to build common cause.

- *Structure teams and accountability.* People perform best in teams connected by a common theory of change. For decision making, organizers need to be accountable to leaders, and leaders need to be accountable to one another and to other supporters.

- *Pick power-building goals, evaluate, and repeat.* Put issues through a power analysis before acting. Learn from successes and failures through reflection and evaluation. Then do it again to keep building.

chapter 2

Digital and Data

We shape our tools and thereafter our tools shape us.

– Marshall McLuhan

Recently, my ten-year-old son had a friend over at our house. This friend happened to walk into my office and reached for my old-school computer monitor. After pressing on the screen a few times with no result, he immediately lost interest and moved on to find something else to do. To him, it was either a touch screen or the equivalent of a useless rock. I've since thought of this moment as a metaphor of where we find ourselves as a society. We've moved from the era of the screen to the era of the touch screen, from more passive consumers of information to more active participants in what we choose to see and whether we want to pass it along to others via social networks. This is part of the breakdown of the broadcast era, but the process is by no means complete and in many ways we are still feeling our way through new realities, with our kids sometimes serving as clues of what is emerging.

Organizers who cut their teeth before the turn of the millennium are often skeptical of and sometimes hostile to the influence of the Internet on campaigns.[1] Conversely, digital natives for whom the Internet has always existed often have little experience systematically building face-to-face relationships offline to get something done. The result is an unhelpful standoff, when in fact the marriage of the two offers exciting opportunities. It doesn't need to be either/or, but can be both – and, with the added incentive that the latter is more likely to win. Often it is political party actors who pioneer this fusion since they get more frequent and disciplined feedback in the form of elections and are therefore highly motivated to innovate and draw from everywhere. NGOs and unions are learning from them and catching up.

Digital tools and practices and good data management do not "change everything" and by themselves do not build real power. At the same time, there is truth in the statement that if your campaign is not on people's smartphones, then for a growing number of people it simply doesn't exist. Good organizers will sort through what they need to adapt and what they need to keep constant. This chapter explores how digital tools and practices and data are altering the landscape for campaigns and opening doors for different kinds of organizing before turning to case studies of two new digital groups – Open Media and SumOfUs – to learn how they succeed at their work. A case study of the Dogwood Initiative explores how it has constantly updated its tech systems to help scale up its organizing. The focus here is less on specific digital tools or channels, which change and go out of date faster than the speed of book publishing, and more on understanding the shift in campaign logic and opportunities.

Old Realities, New Realities

There are reasons to be skeptical about the impact of the Internet on campaigns. The early days of the Internet brought sweeping claims that it would bring "organizing without organizations," bigger and more diverse campaigns with lower barriers to entry, and a means of cheap and distributed coordination without leaders. People would spontaneously self-organize to fix problems and to create solutions. Indeed, there are examples of seemingly spontaneous and leaderless uprisings made possible by digital tools, from the Arab Spring revolts, to the Spanish Indignados protests, to Occupy Wall Street.

Yet, as fast as these popular uprisings grow, they fade away and have mixed results. A new dictator replaced the old dictator in Egypt. Occupy helped to put inequality on the public agenda but then disappeared. In Spain, a new political party with a charismatic leader was needed to focus and continue the energy of the Indignados. It turns out that organizing without organizations is hard to sustain and even harder to turn into an effective force to confront real power. Zeynep Tufekci, a scholar of the Arab Spring and Occupy movements, concludes that "digital infrastructure helps undertake functions that would have otherwise required more formal and long-term organizing which, almost as a side effect, help build organizational capacity to respond to long-term movement requirements."[2] The Internet cannot replace the need for deeper relationship building and leadership, ingredients critical to success.

The question of power underlies much of the debate about the role of digital tools and data in campaigns. Some argue that there is now a challenge from the "new power" of more digital participatory networks to the "old power" hoarded like currencies by the elite.[3] Under this theory, examples of new power actors include Occupy, Wikipedia, and Kickstarter, while examples of old power include the US National Security Agency, the Nobel Prize, and Apple with its top-down design style. If power is framed this way, then we all want to be rooting for the more participatory new power. After all, who wants to be old and undemocratic? But we need to check our assumptions about how we wish the world would work versus how it actually does work.

Just because there is a general trend toward participatory networks doesn't mean that every such network builds power, even defined simply as the ability to act, let alone defined as the ability to act in the face of entrenched interests. In a loose network, people can participate more easily, but whether they do or not, and whether they do at the right time and in the right way, are fluid and uncertain, thus undermining the network's ability to act. And, though it is relatively easy to contribute to Wikipedia or to spend time camping at Zuccotti Park (ground zero for Occupy), it is harder to formulate and agree to a joint strategy and then to change that strategy repeatedly when confronted by a determined opponent, all while maintaining solidarity. Meanwhile old power, like currency (and especially currency), is still effectively hoarded and spent strategically to serve the interests of its owners. Old power is still powerful today and will be tomorrow. New power will need to be better organized if it is to live up to its name and if it hopes to compete with old power. Overall, it's true that "information technology mediates and modifies power relationships; it does not overthrow them."[4] What we see is more a digital evolution than a digital revolution.

Yet something fundamental has changed as we enter the digital era, with profound implications for organizers. Even critics of the Internet acknowledge the magnitude of the shift under way, comparing it with the changes brought on by the printing press.[5] Those who see the Internet or smartphones as mere tools miss the more fundamental changes that are shifting society and will increasingly determine how campaigns are won or lost.

At the most basic level, we are changing our relationship with information. The broadcast era reduced people to passive consumers of information fed through a limited number of TV and radio channels and newspapers. This corresponded to the time that sociologist Theda Skocpol described as a shift "from membership to management,"[6] as people withdrew from direct participation in civic bodies and instead became writers of cheques to politicians or advocacy groups or, in the case of union members, docile payers of dues to the executive. As the Internet and particularly social media displace traditional media, however, "it restores agency to users, enabling active and interactive capacities, in contrast to what with radio, television, and film was a one-way disposition of passive consumption."[7] We see specific pieces of information now because we play a greater role in choosing them. This is the shift from the TV screen to the touch screen, and it establishes at least a participatory orientation toward information, even if people don't always act on it, overwhelmed as they are by volume and variety. When people do participate and share information, they create and reinforce their personal networks, just as they might have done in the past with close friends or colleagues but now at a greater scale, frequency, and visibility on digital channels with larger numbers of people. This has given rise to what some call the "networked society."[8]

The shift is visible in the disruption of traditional media. Between 1995 and 2014, paid daily newspaper circulation fell from about 50 percent of Canadian households to about 20 percent.[9] By 2014, younger Canadians watched about half as much traditional television as older Canadians, preferring to go online instead.[10] About a quarter of Canadian households now have no cable TV, and the rate of disconnecting cable service is growing.[11]

Traditional media are still dominant, and indeed adapting to online channels, but they have less control over boundaries of information than they once had. People are not just online more at home but are also going mobile themselves. Between 2005 and 2015, cellphones overtook landlines in Canadian households,[12] and by 2015 Canadians spent a majority of their digital time on mobile devices rather than on home computers, with those under thirty-five logging two-thirds of their digital time on mobile devices.[13] With the ubiquity of smartphones, people now have few boundaries to information flow no matter where they are. This also means that others can connect with them easily too.

When information is anything, everywhere, and anytime, and when people are making their own choices about what to watch, read, and share, they are "living with, in, and around information ... The idea is that you are living in a stream: adding to it, consuming it, redirecting it."[14] This also changes people's expectations about information sources, whether they are media outlets, companies, institutions, or campaigns. Transparency, interactivity, and responsiveness are now not just expected but also assumed.[15] We see this playing out as all manner of institutions and companies retool to accommodate new expectations. Gone are the days of paternalistic management of customers or citizens. Yet not everyone has moved beyond the broadcast era, and not everyone is demanding responsiveness from institutions, which are changing in reaction to a shifting centre of gravity. Grandparents might still be on the couch watching TV, but enough people in younger generations are now demanding more, and this demand shifts the entire system.

The rise of authenticity is a key part of this trend. Passive consumers have little stake in the information presented to them, and pretty or clever packaging is used to gain acceptance or enthusiasm. The authority of the source matters in that context, too, with expert opinion valued. This was the mode of the broadcast era. But more active participants interacting with information have more of a stake in it, more of a relationship with it, so they prefer something real over something packaged. Active participants do not want to be duped or managed. So, with a new premium on authenticity, political candidates are rewarded for "being themselves," warts and all. This makes politicians such as Rob Ford more viable. Another example is the field of marketing, in which good customer experience has replaced flashy designs or catchy taglines as the way to satisfy customers.[16] It is as much the process as the product.

There is a downside to this shift. The election of Donald Trump as US president in 2016 brought into sharp focus our loss of societal arbiters of truth. The broadcast era lacked a diversity of information channels but also limited the impact of information channels with suspect standards of veracity. We trusted Tom Brokaw or Peter Mansbridge to sort out what was true and what wasn't and to tell us. But the 2016 US election included blatantly fake news stories about the candidates spreading widely through social networks. It also highlighted the phenomenon of the "filter bubble," in which social media platforms play into the hard-wired human tendency to prioritize information that confirms our existing biases by showing only the information that conforms to our ideological bubbles. We might now have a more participatory orientation to information, but the environment in which that orientation occurs encourages us to be more insular and to shut ourselves off more from information that might challenge our assumptions.

A more fluid, participatory environment has accelerated the trend away from people buying membership cards for groups or campaigns of any kind. Membership in political parties has been declining across most of the world. Membership in interest groups has also been declining in North America.[17] A 2013 survey of 2,600 millennials (born between 1980 and 1994) found that they supported causes rather than the institutions working to address them and that 73 percent of them volunteered.[18] Younger citizens are seeking a form of self-expression when they participate, and this can complicate acting together if there is little consensus on direction.[19] Increasingly, support for a group or a campaign is demonstrated by consistently doing things in concert with an organization or a campaign rather than by belonging via a membership card. Allegiances are based upon ongoing merit rather than identity.

Implications for Campaigns

What does weakening of the broadcast era in the face of the digital evolution mean for campaigns? That people have a more participatory orientation to information, institutions, and campaigns is potentially an opportunity for organizing. Today "the digital-media environment prompts new and un-foreseen opportunities for collective action as people are increasingly immersed in an atmosphere in which it is their routine practice to share ideas, connection[s], and interests."[20] In the broadcast era, campaigns needed to overcome stronger boundaries between the public sphere and the private sphere in order to connect, with people hidden safely away in their living rooms and with few readily available indicators of common interest or cause.[21] Campaigns were forced to overcome these stronger boundaries through earned or paid media or through resource-intensive phoning or door-knocking programs. Those boundaries are now weaker, signals of possible interest are now more visible online, and potential supporters are more socially networked, providing the opportunity to bring along groups of like-minded people.

Today, if a campaign is good at entering the digital information stream alongside potential supporters, listening well, and providing appropriate avenues for participation, then it can more easily identify a community to organize into a constituency. But this doesn't happen automatically. It is still work, because "digital media by themselves do not guarantee an audience, a following and, most significantly, they do not guarantee *solidarity*."[22] There is huge competition online not just to gain people's attention but also to hold it, particularly with so much volume and distraction. Should a campaign succeed in making a connection, it is first with a single person. To get to a place of power, to have the ability to act collectively, that person needs to form a common cause with others and to stick with it during inevitable twists and turns in campaigns. This might happen occasionally online with compelling content and with opportunities to participate digitally, particularly on social media, where interactions with others can take place, but it usually happens when the campaign enhances the conversation on the phone or in person. A verbal conversation can establish a more human connection and differentiate the campaign from the dozens of others out there. It is in person, though, that solidarity emerges, and like-minded people form lasting relationships with one another and deliberate on what to do together while developing leadership.

In this more fluid environment, in which tools change quickly and shape preferences, a good campaign will not have static models of engagement. "Rather than offering fixed and inflexible templates for involvement, organizations offer much broader opportunities for people to define their roles and to establish their own participatory styles than one might have imagined."[23] This is not to say, however, that there is no structure. Chapter 3 outlines some flexible campaign structures that both accommodate people's growth inside campaigns and provide avenues for empowerment and accountability.

As campaigns more readily identify like-minded people online, they can redefine the community to help organize it into a constituency. In the past, forging solidarity took place mainly in personal networks that existed or were created in a neighbourhood, a workplace, or a similarly bound geographical unit. Now people who share a community of interest can more easily find one another and form a common cause, even across great distances. Geography still matters, though, since people have fewer opportunities to forge strong solidarity with one another if they are too scattered. But some groups do a good job of identifying a community of interest online and providing opportunities to get together in person once a critical mass is reached. The marriage of digital tools and in-person organizing is the heart of engagement organizing.

Because digital information is now moving so quickly and forcing traditional media to keep up, campaign issue cycles also move more quickly. This is a real challenge for traditional campaigns used to careful research and deliberation, not just because they might lag behind the issue cycle, but also because there are now nimbler competitors quick to step into the vacuum and give supporters another place to go. Or supporters themselves might attempt to self-organize using digital tools. In the NGO sector, this speed has given rise to digital issue generalists who react to news as it happens and provide pathways for people to engage online. There is a healthy debate about the effectiveness of this approach, which critics call "clicktivism," but it's a question of context. If e-petitions and hashtags are ends in themselves, then little power will be built, and good digital groups are highly aware of this. If these tactics are just the starting point of engagement, however, then there are opportunities to build solidarity and to do more together. Regardless, information flows and issue cycles are not going to return to a more leisurely pace. Campaigns will either speed up or be left behind.

Digital tools not only enable easier group formation, leading to more competition for attention and relevance, but also reduce coordination costs for all groups. Email was born during the early days of the Internet and is still an inexpensive workhorse for either small group deliberations or mass e-blasts to announce events or other campaign happenings. Voice and video are now carried online for cheap or free, enabling richer conversations between leaders and/or supporters. Newer online apps provide helpful structures for online group collaboration and project management to enable a high-functioning relationship with the person in the next cubicle or the next country. Powerful off-the-shelf database systems can serve many information needs in one place at low cost. High overhead for brick-and-mortar offices and work systems is increasingly unnecessary. Even the pre-Internet Alinsky kept this line written on his office blackboard: "Low Overhead = High Independence."[24] Campaigns can take advantage of these cost savings to shift resources to their front-line work.

Overall, the implications of the erosion of the broadcast era for campaigns are disruption and opportunity. The Internet has already significantly disrupted how people relate to information, and institutions are undergoing a sea change to become more transparent and responsive. Networks among people are now larger, more active, and more visible thanks to digital tools. The shift is still under way, so it's hard to make firm conclusions about how things will work even a year from now. Campaigns need to keep adapting or cede ground to more numerous and more nimble competitors. On the opportunity side, there has never been a time when a constituency has been as easy to find and communicate with. What happens next, though, is what matters. There might be extraordinary times when people self-organize at scale around a goal using digital tools, but these uprisings will be both infrequent and ephemeral. Alternatively, organizers can use this opportunity to form relationships and to help stitch people together into structures of solidarity using community organizing principles. One difference now is that communities of interest can more easily transcend geography and scale more quickly. This makes engagement organizing possible.

Data, Measurement, and Testing

Digital tools didn't create data and measurement, but they have facilitated a new culture of data management and testing. The average person can keep track of up to 200 relationships in her or his head.[25] Beyond that, tools are needed, such as paper and pen, a spreadsheet, or a database. Today a database is a campaign's most important asset after its people. It is the campaign's brain. Campaigns have always used data – even the most basic grassroots campaign will have phone lists of key contacts. Today, though, digital innovations have made data tools both more powerful and more accessible. Even low-budget campaigns can now afford data management once accessible only to those with lots of resources.

As recently as ten years ago, if a campaign wanted access to a useful database, it had to hire programmers to build one in-house and run it on its own hardware. As technology got better, companies such as Salesforce began to develop off-the-shelf database products that campaigns could pay for and customize. Databases went from being big capital expenses to being routine and affordable operating costs. American presidential campaigns, particularly Democratic ones, innovated further by creating new data systems for organizing and after the dust settled spun off systems such as Blue State Digital, tailored to campaign needs and available to progressive organizations. Eventually, companies such as NationBuilder put out systems that could be accessed relatively cheaply by anyone. (Americans tend to see such tech systems in partisan terms, and NationBuilder has faced controversy for being available to anyone, including Trump.) These systems collect and store data, run websites and petitions, integrate with social media and texting, facilitate financial transactions, issue canvass walks and calling lists, and provide different levels of access to campaign members, all in the same place and all for a low price. The significance is how it has levelled the playing field between campaigns with money and those without.

There is no longer an insurmountable barrier for any campaign to have good data management. The biggest challenges lie with organizations that existed before these new tools became available and that now have data scattered in multiple systems that can't do what's needed by modern campaigns. Migrating and cleaning data are a headache but unavoidable if groups want to be effective. The accessibility and functionality of the tools enable better data practices beyond simply gathering and storing data properly. These practices and methods can quickly become technical and intimidating to those not immersed in that world, but they come down to four overall functions:

1   *Tracking.* Effective campaigners are serious about keeping track of people's relationships to the campaigns. Every event can make signing in a condition of entry. Every mass email can be monitored for who opens it and who clicks on which links. Every donation can be logged. But data that don't get entered don't exist. Ideally, different kinds of data are stored in a single repository so that campaigners can paint a complete picture of every supporter.

2   *Segmentation.* Different people do different things in campaigns and should be communicated with accordingly. Volunteers can be separated from general supporters and people in one city from those in another. Supporters with similar interests can be segmented from supporters with other interests. Campaigns are more powerful when they communicate with people in a way they want to be communicated with.

3   *Targeting.* When a campaign doesn't know a person and how she or he will react to a communication, it can make an educated guess based upon data. Where a person lives, what census data say about the area, and whether or not the person is a member of a club can all be brought together to inform campaign decisions about spending limited time or resources. Larger and more sophisticated campaigns might have enough data and enough outreach capacity to engage in micro-targeting of small subsets of potential supporters or even assigning probabilistic scores to every person of interest to guide communication. All campaigns, though, can make smarter choices about where to allocate limited time or money.

4   *Testing and evaluation.* This begins with asking "What works best?" and trying to answer the question objectively through measurement and experimentation. New digital tools make it easy to test multiple versions of emails and other communications to discover which ones perform best – often known as "A/B testing." Simple measurement and evaluation can be applied to most things that a campaign does. With planning, more rigorous randomized experiments can be designed to evaluate campaign options. Overall, campaigns can use data for constant evaluation to become more effective, and the best ones do.

Depending on the complexity of the data task and the resources available to a campaign, experts can be hired to help with this kind of work. But basic segmentation, targeting, and testing and evaluation can be done by all campaigns for no or low cost beyond the investment of time. Good data management is more a cultural than a technical exercise, and it can help campaigns to become stronger. Data, though, are not a silver bullet. There has been a lot of hype about "Big Data," particularly following the Obama presidential campaigns when their sophisticated data practices were widely reported on and held up as a critical ingredient. But data are not a campaign. They can only help your other activities – communicating, organizing, fundraising – to become stronger and better integrated. Data do not replace organizing but can enhance it. Perhaps the biggest counterpoint to Big Data was the 2016 Trump campaign in the United States in which the candidate famously eschewed data and won anyway. His opponent, Hillary Clinton, embraced data modelling to such a degree that her campaign became inflexible and unable to adapt in the face of a changing landscape.[26]

A recent example of the use of data and predictive modelling in a campaign is the 2016 contest for mayor of Saskatoon.[27] Contender Charlie Clark knew that he couldn't spend much money to try to defeat incumbent Don Atchison, since spending rules capped each campaign at about $200,000 – slightly less than a dollar per elector. Clark's campaign did have a good number of volunteers, though, and organizers began to figure out which voters those volunteers should focus on talking to in their limited time. The campaign built a database of electors and used demographic data and a poll to create predictive scores for everyone on the list. Up to 35 percent of the electorate was excluded from phoning and foot-canvassing lists as the campaign filtered its database using combinations of ten "buckets" of voters, ranging from those predicted to be most supportive to those less so. As the campaign progressed, it used canvassing and phone banking to test and refine the scores, and then it concentrated on the best buckets of voters during GOTV (get out the vote) work on election day. Clark defeated Atchison by 41 to 37 percent, even though public polls during the campaign showed him lagging behind his opponent in all but the eighteen-to-thirty-four age group.[28]

With the increasing pervasiveness of data and the ability to act on them with digital tools, ethical issues arise, and campaigns need to pay attention to them. Without the right attitudes and practices, when we systematically collect information on people, we can treat them as objects to be managed instead of persons with agency. The best antidote is making supporters aware of how they are showing up in data streams and why that matters to a campaign. Most democracies have laws governing privacy that require organizations and campaigns to be responsive to people's wishes about being in a database and to protect personal information. Organizations can go further, though, by checking in repeatedly with supporters about data practices. This pays off not just in managing data ethics but also in fostering more buy in to the work in general. The alternative is mistrust and loss of potential supporters.

Case Studies

Here I focus on two large Canada-wide digital groups and one BC group leading the way on both engagement organizing and the tech systems that support it. Many digital groups owe a debt to the US progressive group MoveOn.org, which pioneered many of the practices seen today. Some call these practices "digital organizing," but they are better termed "digital mobilizing" unless there is a consistent effort to move supporters into forging solidarity with one another and giving them campaign responsibilities. MoveOn was created in 1998 by two Silicon Valley tech entrepeneurs tired of the Clinton-Lewinsky affair. They encouraged Americans to just "move on" through an online petition, a new tactic at the time. Half a million people signed the petition, and when that alone didn't achieve the desired result MoveOn asked signatories to become active, and they did. Thus was born the model of identifying people online (through an initial easy request such as signing a petition) and then engaging them further. In 2002, MoveOn pivoted to oppose the Iraq War and became an issue generalist, taking on various hot-button topics as they arose and creating a new model in the process.

Groups such as MoveOn have given rise to a debate about "clicktivism" and whether the constant signing of e-petitions is at best ineffective and at worst counterproductive since it fosters disillusionment by people who care but see no progress after signing. But what comes next matters. Some groups, MoveOn included, provide more pathways for engagement, including offline. MoveOn has local councils for supporters to work together face to face and hires field organizers to support them. Other online groups join in coalitions with other types of organizations to build enough power to win.

Open Media: An Online Coalition Partner

Steve Anderson took a series of odd jobs to fund his dream of creating an independent media outlet.[29] He was once so bored writing a setup guide for a new software company that he took the picture of a horse on the front of the software package and did the whole guide in the voice of the horse. "Gallop on over and press the shift key," he wrote. From those beginnings ten years ago, today Open Media has over 600,000 Canadians on its email list and has helped to win several battles related to Internet access and privacy, changing the nature of the Canadian telecom regulator in the process.[30] Open Media is predominantly an online organization and a good case study of what's possible in a new digital environment.

As Anderson describes it, Open Media is Canada's immune system for the Internet, and it works globally given that the Internet does. It has three pillars of work: making the Internet accessible to all, safeguarding privacy against online surveillance, and standing up for free expression online. Before launching Open Media, Anderson went to the United States and worked with groups active on Internet freedom. There he learned an approach to coalition networks that would be instrumental to his later work. Battling big telecom companies requires multiple groups coming together to build power.

In 2008, Bell Canada started slowing down the ability of the Canadian Broadcasting Corporation to stream some of its videos online, and the Canadian campaign for net neutrality was born. The Save Our Net coalition came together and succeeded in convincing Ottawa to pass some of the strongest open Internet rules in the world. About 9,000 people engaged through an online petition that Anderson managed. In 2010–11, things exploded. The telecom companies came forward with a plan to introduce Internet metering, prompting fears that online access would become unaffordable for many. Through a new online petition, Open Media's list doubled within a week and went to half a million within a few months. This was the largest online campaign in Canadian history.

When the national regulator – the Canadian Radio-Television and Telecommunications Commission (CRTC) – sided with the telecom companies, Open Media turned to its online community to seek advice and ask it to weigh in. There was a surge in creativity as supporters made graphics, videos, and even a hip-hop song. They participated in rallies and contacted politicians. Appropriately, the minister in charge used Twitter to tell the CRTC to go back to the drawing board. At hearings that followed, Open Media helped 100,000 people to make submissions, and it crowd-sourced the testimony that Anderson gave. The CRTC backed down.

Anderson describes a democratic deficit that exists in many of our institutions. If the CRTC was doing what Canadians wanted, it wouldn't make as many bad decisions, but it has trouble listening. When Anderson testified with the stories that Canadians had provided to him, the chair of the CRTC said that the stories were out of scope. Anderson wondered how a regulator could be so dismissive of the public in a public hearing. After a backlash, the chair was replaced, and the first act of the new chair was to meet with Open Media. At his first hearing, the new chair himself read out citizens' comments for the record. The CRTC is now somewhat more democratic, but as Anderson says "we had to kick the door open and hold it there."

To keep track of its 600,000 supporters, Open Media pays for access to a database system and uses open-source software to create a dashboard to manage it. Volunteers stepped forward to build an online letter-to-the-editor tool. You enter your postal code, and a list of local newspapers pops up. You choose which ones to send your letter to, click, and off it goes. Open Media does A/B testing on things such as email subject lines, templates, and some variations in language. It tracks metrics in various ways, including through an "appeal resonance rate" that combines email open rates with actions taken so that it can see what's working and what's not. Metrics are bundled up on a weekly, quarterly, and annual basis and fed into decision making.

Consistent with its mandate, Open Media crowd-sources everything it can, itself modelling how to overcome the democratic deficit. Position papers are written using an online tool that lets supporters drag and drop principles and policies to rank and filter them. Before important meetings or testimonies, the online community is asked what should be said, and a report is given afterward. Its social media coordinator responds to comments and brings relevant online feedback to weekly staff meetings. Petition signers aren't asked for a membership fee but are considered supporters unless they unsubscribe. Open Media works with a five-stage "pyramid of engagement," trying to move people toward broader and deeper engagement, from a single e-petition, to more e-petitions, to writing letters, to donating, to showing up for events, and to crowd-sourcing policy positions. People at level five are considered part of the digital action team and are asked to do more complex things, such as host events. About 60 percent of the organization's budget comes from individual donations, which keeps Open Media accountable to its supporters and gives it the freedom to work on what needs to be done rather than on what large donors might want to be done.

Open Media knows that it cannot go it alone. It engages in network coalitions in which agreements are struck with other groups on what they are for or against, with any coalition member free to pursue that outcome using the tactics at which the coalition is best. Anderson is fond of participating in cross-partisan coalitions, as he did on privacy issues surrounding the Conservative government's Bill C-51, when Open Media worked with right-leaning groups such as the Canadian Taxpayers Federation, the National Firearms Association, and the Dominion Institute.

One difference that separates Open Media from some online rapid response organizations is that it is less rapid. With a more circumscribed mandate, it digs in deeper on its issues and might need to stay with them for longer periods. Open Media worked quietly for six months on Bill C-30, which would have expanded government online surveillance, before the minister of public safety exploded the issue by saying that opponents of the bill were on the side of child pornographers. Open Media stood ready and capitalized on the outcry, eventually helping to kill the legislation.

A challenge that Open Media faces is establishing a set of values that holds its supporters together. People might have come into its online community through an action on one of its three pillars (access, privacy, free expression), but they might have little affinity for the other two. A person who cares about cheap Internet access, for example, might not be interested in privacy. The answer, as Anderson sees it, is for Open Media to articulate a compelling set of values that binds supporters together. Ultimately, it's about participatory democracy and openness, bigger picture things on which many people can agree. In its eight-year history, Open Media has used the Internet to engage hundreds of thousands of Canadians in protecting it. Its use of digital tools, its leadership of network coalitions, and its genuine commitment to bottom-up decision making have made it an online model.

SumOfUs: Providing Surge Capacity

Liz McDowell was one of many Canadians heartbroken by the failure of the Copenhagen climate conference in 2009.[31] She identified with the argument that the power of entrenched corporate interests was standing in the way of progress. Counterbalancing that power wherever it exists globally was the mission of a then new online organization called SumOfUs,[32] for which McDowell now serves as campaign director. The growth of SumOfUs has been nothing short of meteoric. After only four years, its global list is about 5 million, with about 600,000 of that number in Canada.

SumOfUs is a multi-issue rapid response organization. It jumps on hot-button issues of the day if they are consistent with its mandate to challenge corporate power, at various scales from the local to the national to the global. An existing or potential supporter will be given the opportunity to sign an online petition and then to share it with friends and colleagues through email or social media. McDowell believes that SumOfUs works best by providing "surge capacity" at key moments as part of joint efforts with other groups. In 2015, for example, it joined several organizations fighting the giveaway of BC groundwater to companies such as Nestlé under new provincial regulations. About 200,000 people signed a petition, creating both an online buzz and offline media stories and helping to convince the government to review its regulations.

SumOfUs will occasionally go to its list to fundraise for allies. It successfully raised tens of thousands of dollars for First Nations in British Columbia fighting international trade agreements and pipeline projects. The lesson about not going it alone is underlined by a story. In 2014, SumOfUs took on Canadian oil giant Suncor for running a public relations campaign claiming to be a responsible actor while lobbying against new water regulations in Alberta. SumOfUs ran a petition and spoofed Suncor's public relations materials, bringing the company to the table. But, without allies providing campaign consistency, SumOfUs found it hard to sustain the focus. Its rapid response logic moved it on to other issues before a resolution was found.

SumOfUs is global but has regional teams, with one for North America that includes Canadian campaigners. A person who signs a petition in Canada will be exposed to other issues in the country as well as to global petitions. There is no membership fee, but the organization tracks what it calls the "member journey." This consists of a new supporter getting a series of welcome emails explaining more about what SumOfUs does. People are then asked to share a video, call a CEO or politician, or donate money. Borrowing a tactic pioneered by MoveOn, SumOfUs is experimenting with allowing its supporters to start their own petitions through its website. If one of these petitions does well, then the organization will consider sending it to its list if the issue is within its mission. One of its most successful supporter-generated petitions, though, was about social security for teachers, which wasn't close enough to its mission to actively support.

With about 5 million people on its global email list, SumOfUs pays close attention to data. It avoids what it calls "vanity metrics," such as overall list size, in favour of metrics that tell it something about its power to achieve change. It developed a measure called "members returning for action," which measures the number of people taking action in any given month to indicate whether it is designing compelling actions that are easy to take. A refinement is a metric called the "reactivation rate," which measures on a rolling basis the number of people taking action who have not taken action in the past thirty or sixty days. SumOfUs is also looking at longer-term issues of the health of its network. One issue concerns email fatigue. How many emails can supporters receive for how long before their actions drop off, particularly donations? It is running experiments on this issue over a period of six to nine months, a long time for an online group.

One worry relates to changes that Facebook has made to its display algorithms. Like other online groups, SumOfUs achieved much of its early growth through supporters sharing its petitions on Facebook. With the growth of Facebook, there is now so much content competing for limited space in the news feed that people only see the content that their friends are most strongly engaged with and sharing. Petitions of all kinds can therefore get less play. New social platforms, apps, and texting tools are always emerging, and SumOfUs is looking at what's next on this front. At the time of writing, it pays for access to ActionKit, an online action system developed by the team that helped to build the technology for MoveOn. The system integrates website management, online petitions, social media, data management, and more. SumOfUs constantly evaluates its technology to see how it can be improved as new functions become available.

Although McDowell likes the fact that the multi-issue, rapid response model means that there is something for everyone, she worries that it can feel a bit "scatty," with one issue today, another issue tomorrow, and reporting back on the first one the next day. SumOfUs is working on developing its voice, on finding a cohesive narrative that it can use to tie things together and keep people engaged. Overall, SumOfUs shows the rapidity with which digital mobilization can scale up today as well as the strengths and limitations of a mostly digital model and how they can be managed.

Dogwood Initiative, Part 1: Organizing Systems

The Victoria-based Dogwood Initiative has a mission to help British Columbians reclaim power over their environment and democracy.[33] Dogwood is different from Open Media and SumOfUs in that it goes beyond digital mobilizing into full-scale organizing with supporters. In fact, Dogwood is one of the earliest adopters of engagement organizing in Canada, and as such it is one of the most sophisticated actors in the field. But it wasn't always this way. Dogwood began as an advocacy group without a theory of change that directly engages supporters at scale. As such, its evolution is a fascinating case study. Here I focus on its systems and data. In the next chapter, I look at its campaign cycle.

Matt Takach joined Dogwood in 2007, fresh from the world of party politics in which he was used to the culture of lists.[34] When he joined Dogwood, it was using spreadsheets to manage its few contacts, with an old database that was largely abandoned. The group's website ran on Plone, an open-source content management system, which at that point couldn't handle basic e-petitions. If Dogwood was serious about growing its support base, then its systems needed to change, but the organization had almost no budget for that.

Luckily, a non-profit group in Seattle had the mandate to help environmental groups across the Pacific Northwest to upgrade their systems and strategies. It developed an app for Plone called Megaphone that enabled e-petitions. Critically, it also developed tools and practices to adapt the sophisticated commercial database system Salesforce for use by non-profits. The good news is that Megaphone syncs automatically with Salesforce so that groups don't have to transfer data manually. Dogwood then added some segmentation by geography so that it could communicate with all of its supporters in a riding or even within a polling division. The group now had the ability to recruit people online and to track the data systematically in a robust back end.

Karl Hardin came on board in 2009 to work in communications and quickly gravitated to digital work.[35] He updated the website from what he called an "atrocious *New York Times* three-column format" and optimized it for email capture. Dogwood was reposting news articles to its website to drive traffic until the news outlets cracked down on copyright issues and forced the organization to rely more heavily on its own blog content. Hardin also spent much time troubleshooting the buggy email distribution tool run by a small San Francisco company. Sometimes he called it every day.

Dogwood became better at digital campaigning. It aggressively drove e-petitions and developed what it calls a "drip" series of automatically sent emails to welcome online supporters. The first follow-up email after somebody signs an e-petition says thank you and articulates Dogwood's mission and values. The second a few days later is a fundraising pitch. The third a few days after that contains Dogwood's most recent e-newsletter. The drip series helps to condition supporters to the communications that they will receive longer term. Dogwood experimented with recruitment in the early days of Facebook. Hardin would target ads to people who liked the pages of other NGOs to fish for new supporters. In what he considers to be his "first big moment in digital," he wrote code to enable supporters to send a fax off Dogwood's website to the National Energy Board to oppose an oil pipeline. Over 1,400 people did so and helped to spark a backlash from the Canadian government that turbocharged the campaign.

Up to this point, Dogwood had been mobilizing rather than organizing, and this was reflected in its tools. As the group shifted toward having its supporters lead the charge, it needed an evolution of its tech tools. Trial and error would teach it much. Hardin spent a lot of time in Plone developing a sequence of pages to walk a keen supporter through a process that it called "Find Leaders." The pages coached supporters on how to contact decision makers and to work with other volunteers. The whole initiative was slow and unwieldy and ultimately abandoned. Hardin thought that he learned an important lesson: focus on the people first instead of the tools. But it would take another mistake for the lesson to sink in fully.

Tech nerds everywhere were inspired by the 2012 Obama campaign toolset, and Dogwood set about to replicate the Dashboard system that Obama volunteers used. Hardin thought that Dogwood could adapt the NationBuilder platform to do so. In the buildup to the 2013 BC election, Hardin and his team set up twenty-two mini content management systems within NationBuilder so that volunteers could work together in twenty-two target ridings. This gave leaders specialized access to potential volunteer lists and tools for volunteer management. Hardin and four others spent two days in a room manually setting up NationBuilder in a process that has since been mostly automated. But, after all this work, only a few people used the systems. Once again Dogwood had prioritized tools over people. "Like *Field of Dreams* we thought if we build it they will come," said Hardin. "It didn't turn out to be the case."

Dogwood was more committed than ever to becoming "an organizing superpower," so Hardin worked with the field team to fix things. They stuck with NationBuilder as a volunteer hub and streamlined it. Most importantly, when somebody signed up to volunteer, Dogwood now required that person to fill in a phone number, and the group implemented the practice of a follow-up phone call within five days. The philosophy was "how to get a phone number to get humans talking to each other and use digital tools to facilitate those interactions." Dogwood set up local and regional teams and automated the passing along of phone numbers for follow-up to volunteer leaders who emerged. Its conversion rates jumped. Dogwood supplied training on NationBuilder to leaders with webinars and through a dedicated support person.

The group had made good progress, but there were still problems. It still had a Plone website even though the user community had diminished, with developers becoming rarer compared with similar systems such as WordPress. "I joke that if I were to throw a rock right now I'd have a pretty good chance of hitting a WordPress developer," said Hardin. "But if I want to hit a Plone developer I'd have to take a ferry to Seattle and knock on one specific door and then throw the rock." Dogwood had always been busy chasing campaign cycles and had never had the time and space to step back and shift to something else. "Imagine building a house and never maintaining it – that's what we did with Plone," said Takach. Dogwood had also been using NationBuilder for e-petitions, with the problem that the system didn't synchronize with

Salesforce. This led to bottlenecks and loss of staff time as data were manually transferred.

Dogwood's "tech stack" has always been evolving, and at the time of writing it has come together better than ever before. For its website, it is now using WordPress, which is more user friendly and will enable easier testing of landing pages for optimizing signups. It is using Marketo for email blasts, and it synchronizes easily with Salesforce. It uses NationBuilder as its volunteer hub and has written code to automatically synchronize data from there with Salesforce. For phone banking, it has recently used CallFire, a web-based system that lets volunteers anywhere participate in calling drives, with the resultant data collected in one place. Salesforce has evolved to have a dedicated, non-profit "Starter Pack" with functionality more suited to NGOs. Maggie Gilbert, Dogwood's current Digital Systems and Data Management Team Lead, says that the organization has become wiser about selecting tech tools through trial and error and now asks whether a new tool integrates with others, is well supported, and is being used in its intended way.[36]

DOGWOOD'S "TECH STACK"

Figure 1 This is an oversimplified picture of Dogwood's current "tech stack" – the systems that it uses to do its work. Note that all systems feed into and out of Salesforce, the central database. Dogwood has worked to have the pieces interact with one another without the need for finicky and time-consuming manual data transfer.

Throughout, Dogwood has cultivated a culture of testing. No email gets sent without at least testing subject lines and often variations on content or design. An initial test is sent to groups within a pool of about 30,000 people, and the best-performing email is sent to the rest of the 180,000 on the e-list. The group has segmented its supporter list based upon political geography and engagement. It automatically categorizes its supporters in an engagement pyramid and tailors communications to people on various levels. Dogwood has also started regular surveys of its members to be able to add demographic data.

Dogwood has learned to bring a product management philosophy to its systems work. As Hardin says, much of Dogwood's tech history has been "duct tape and bootstrapping." It now approaches tech tools more intentionally, scoping projects and setting realistic budgets for them. It is also moving to decentralize its tech work, with a new management structure that puts it into the hands of more people in the organization. Through experience, Dogwood has become an expert in applying tech systems to organizing and now consults to other NGOs and political campaigns to share what it has learned. Says Gilbert, "don't be afraid to invest in tech. It may be expensive, but it will be worth it. You don't want to use things that constantly need fixing. That's soul crushing."

Lessons for Engagement Organizing

The Internet, digital and mobile tools, and the use of data don't themselves add up to power, but they have changed how people relate to information and how accessible they are to organizers. Groups and the campaigns that they run are now able to define and reach different and bigger communities more easily and to build constituencies quickly and at scale. Potential supporters have a variety of ways to communicate and an increased expectation of interactivity and authenticity. New campaigns are easier to start and therefore more numerous, leading to more competition for resources, including one of the most precious resources of all: attention.

Campaigns that embrace these changes will have an advantage over those that don't. At the same time, campaigns that rely only on digital tools and tactics will find winning difficult. Supporters must build solidarity offline or forge alliances with groups that bring other kinds of power to the table.

Here are some lessons for engagement organizing from the discussion of digital tools and data:

- *Use digital tools to help define and engage your constituency.* You can now define a bigger community of interest, reach people more easily to help form them into a constituency, and encourage them to interact with the campaign in a diversity of ways.

- *Be nimble around faster issue cycles.* Information is now travelling more quickly, and if you aren't responding to the latest relevant news somebody else is. Decide whether that matters to your campaign.

- *Support relationships with elegant data management.* New systems let you keep all your relationship information in one place. This is your campaign brain – think clearly.

- *Measure, test, and adapt.* Why be good when you could be great? Adopt a culture of asking what works best. Measure campaign tactics and test alternatives. Make changes based upon the results.

- *Recognize the limitations of digital tools and build other power.* Campaigns aren't won online. Use digital tools to create opportunities to build solidarity in person. Build alliances with groups that bring different kinds of leverage to the table.

chapter 3

Scaling and Networked Communications

In the end, we'll all become stories.

– Margaret Atwood

Just after 3 p.m. on the day before the 2015 federal election, Gail Armitage made her last phone call to encourage a citizen to get out and cast a ballot the next day.[1] She was a volunteer not for a political party but for the Dogwood Initiative. Over the prior days and weeks, she had made 602 phone calls and was one of 854 Dogwood volunteers who together had made 42,551 calls. We know this because each call had automatically been logged in a calling software program. Armitage had started volunteering with the organization the prior spring when she had signed up online to oppose the threat of new oil tankers on the BC coast. She had been recruited to join a Dogwood team and had become the team leader. This is an example of an organization engaging volunteers at scale through digital tools, a flexible campaign structure, and networked communications.

The first two chapters established organizing principles and showed how the campaign landscape has changed as digital tools contribute to the breakdown of the broadcast era. Organizations can now identify communities of interest more quickly and at larger scales. Whether this translates into building power depends on the ability to forge solidarity and leadership in those communities, which requires attention to organizing principles. This combination is the heart of engagement organizing. Done right, it allows campaigns to go big at key moments. But it also requires striking a balance. On the one hand, campaigns need to be open to grassroots energy,[2] and they must be willing not only to engage in genuine conversations with potential supporters but also to empower them to talk to one another across their networks, which means some loss of control. On the other hand, campaigns need to stay focused on their goals and not succumb to the chaos of having no structure. This chapter explores some approaches to striking this balance. The "engagement cycle" and "snowflake" structure for distributed leadership can help campaigns to respect and empower supporters while providing necessary structure. Engagement organizing also entails a redefinition of campaign communications toward an approach that recognizes the growing role of networks.

Scaling: The Engagement Cycle and the Snowflake

Engagement organizing is about directly engaging people at scale in causes that they support. This is a process. People come to the campaign with different levels of commitment and experience, both of which can improve with good campaign design. Although there is no one right pathway for every supporter or every campaign, there are some helpful metaphors or models available. In the previous chapter, I discussed the pyramid of engagement of Open Media and the member journey of SumOfUs. Here I explore the models of the engagement cycle and the snowflake.

Models simplify complex phenomena to reveal key qualities. Every model will include something and exclude something. Many organizations use the model of a ladder or pyramid of engagement to structure their relationships with supporters. These models address the concept of segmentation. Supporters have different relationships with a campaign, from being volunteers to being donors, or interest in one issue but not another, and they prefer to interact accordingly. A campaign can be intentional and plan activities to deepen engagement, moving from less commitment to more or from easier contributions to more challenging ones. A good way for a campaign to know if it is making progress is by tracking this movement: does it have more people at higher levels of the ladder than it did a year ago?

THE ENGAGEMENT CYCLE

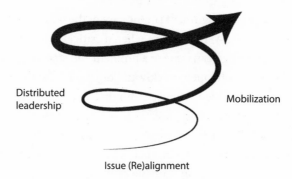

Distributed leadership

Mobilization

Issue (Re)alignment

Figure 2 Engagement organizing has an overlapping, three-phase cycle. People form common cause through issue alignment or realignment during subsequent iterations. Mobilization occurs when they act together to advance their goals. Distributed leadership sees leaders emerge to take responsibility – and accountability – for organizing parts of the work within a shared theory of change. With more iterations, a campaign can scale up.

Here I discuss a cycle of engagement. This model leaves out the concept of segmentation and focuses instead on a desirable rhythm for campaigns. A ladder or a pyramid implies more of a top-down relationship between an organization and a supporter, whereas campaigns today can develop more from the bottom up, emerging from the relationships among supporters themselves, with an organization playing a supporting role. A cycle captures the fluidity of people's engagement, since a supporter might come in as a key leader right away or play a larger role at one moment and a lesser role at another.

As SumOfUs senior campaigner Nicole Carty says, "the traditional ladder of engagement, in which people are encouraged to incrementally scale up their involvement, has little to no bearing [on today's campaigns] – here you can go from 0 to 60 in no time at all, and from 60 to 0 just as quickly."[3] Campaigns need to be open to multiple pathways of engagement and to shifting roles as campaigns evolve. In an engagement organizing cycle, there are three overlapping phases: issue (re)alignment, mobilization, and distributed leadership. The ideal is that as a campaign or an organization does its work, it cycles through these phases and attracts more people and more resources, becoming bigger as it goes. The visual looks like an arrow going in circles and expanding outward and upward.

Issue alignment or realignment (in the case of the next iteration of a campaign or a new campaign) takes place when a critical mass of people agrees on the common framing of an issue or a problem and starts moving to action. In a digital era, this can happen quickly and organically, with people finding one another online and negotiating a common framing to make enough of a commitment to go to the next phase. Or this process can be mediated by an existing organization that provides guidance, particularly if it is perceived as a trusted entity that can help gain success. Even then forging critical mass will be easier if the organization frames a campaign as an invitation as much as a proposition and is genuinely open to incorporating feedback and adapting. Less likely today is a group able to dictate issues and tactics and to expect large-scale pickup. Volunteers will vote either way with their feet and donors with their wallets.

Mobilization tests whether supporters are up for more. Mobilization includes opportunities to engage in higher-effort activities such as showing up for a meeting or performing a task that takes more time or in public events such as a canvass, strike, direct action, or community potluck. Donating to the campaign is also a form of mobilization. Good campaigns will make sure that they are articulating a clear theory of change to mobilize supporters, telling them how their specific contributions are helping to achieve the desired outcome. If a campaign intends to get to distributed leadership, then mobilization will also test for leadership qualities among participants. Leaders will begin to shine.

Distributed leadership goes beyond mobilizing and invests in some key supporters to positively transform their motivations and capacities to step up even more.[4] Organizers identify and develop leaders and support them as they take on responsibilities. This allows a campaign to scale up by having leaders own parts of it and to help organize others. A variation on this model specific to union organizing is to identify and develop "organic" leaders in the place to be organized, meaning those people who already have an informal following based upon their personal relationships and skills, such as the person sought out when a colleague doesn't know how to do something.[5]

Organizers foster distributed leadership development in three ways.[6] First, they bring potential leaders into contact with one another and give them some autonomy. Second, rather than assign small activities that leaders can do alone, organizers work with them to help define larger campaign tasks that leaders can do interdependently with others. Third, organizers develop leaders through training, coaching, and reflection.

Engagement organizing means getting to distributed leadership. Many campaigns skip this phase and just mobilize, not organize. The difference lies in the empowerment of supporters. Mobilization asks supporters to do a task or to give money, whereas in organizing leaders step up to help define campaign tasks and take responsibility for working with others to get those tasks done. Not all supporters want to be leaders, though, and campaigns might prioritize mobilizing over organizing at critical moments when pressure is most needed. The engagement cycle keeps turning, and when a campaign hits a blockage or a plateau issue realignment might be needed to keep things moving. Or an issue might be won or lost, in which case the campaign or group must decide whether to keep going around the cycle, drawing on people already in the network and newcomers to engage once again in issue alignment for a new cycle. A larger group might have different engagement cycles taking place at the same time on different issues.

The need to get to distributed leadership brings us to another metaphor, that of the snowflake. What does a campaign do when a number of supporters step forward and want to do something in person, particularly when there isn't enough staff capacity to interact with each of them? A traditional approach is to try to develop a command-and-control hierarchy, with managers at various levels responsible for other managers, down to the level of volunteers. There are a couple of drawbacks with that model. First, campaigns often need each manager in the chain to be directly under their control and likely paid. There might not be enough resources for that. Second, this model can stifle enthusiasm if people feel that they are being ordered around. Volunteers have less agency and will be less engaged.

Instead, the snowflake model assumes the formation of interdependent teams led by volunteer leaders and supported by the campaign. The interdependence comes from a common overall theory of change, with each team taking on a portion of the work and being held accountable for delivering on it, even as the teams themselves decide how best to act. Each member of a team likewise takes on her or his part and is held accountable by other team members for delivering it. The teams and their members have their

THE SNOWFLAKE MODEL

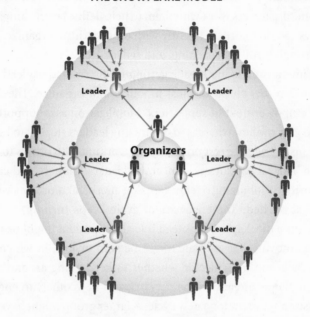

Figure 3 The snowflake is a model for distributed leadership. Organizers support teams of volunteer leaders who in turn support teams of other volunteers to act together within a shared theory of change. The teams hold one another accountable for decisions and for results. No one organizer or team leader manages more than about eight relationships. A snowflake can scale beyond this diagram, with new teams extending from the outer tier of people as they too become leaders. This diagram is based on the work of Marshall Ganz.

own agency to act without always being told what to do but within common goals. The magic takes place in the teams when deeper relationships form based upon acting together. The snowflake "is an effort to create an effective organizational structure that's more collaborative in its foundation than it is authoritarian," says Marshall Ganz.[7] A larger group might have more than one snowflake with multiple issues in play.

Building out a snowflake requires careful consideration of ratios to avoid bottlenecks. An individual team should be comprised of about eight people or fewer so that the team leader doesn't have too many relationships to track and coach. Then eight team leaders or fewer will have one person to coach and coordinate them and so forth. As campaigns grow or shrink, teams can divide or merge or be reconstituted entirely. A team might have an overall leader in addition to several functional leaders, driven by the needs of the campaign. An election campaign, for example, might have team captains for canvassing, phone banking, and data gathering, with several volunteers working with that captain. Or a different kind of campaign might have team captains for research, outreach, and fundraising. Campaigns need to trust their people for distributed leadership to work. There is a certain letting go of control necessary to allow leaders to have their own agency at all tiers of the snowflake. This can be challenging to those used to a conventional command-and-control model.

At each phase of the engagement cycle a key question is "who decides?" Ultimately, supporters are united in a campaign by a shared theory of change, but how it is developed determines whether there is buy in, longevity, and the ability to win. Initial issue alignment and first mobilization can either emerge organically or be planned in a more top-down manner, depending on the situation. If a campaign needs to evolve and scale up, then it will need to grapple with the issues of leadership and accountability. Those who invest significant time in and take responsibility for a part of the campaign need to be included in decision making. Others might not want to take that much on but still participate and are given opportunities to hold leaders accountable. The campaign needs to constantly grapple with the balance between diverse feedback from team leaders and a coherent theory of change.[8] Legitimacy in this model is continuously negotiated and earned.

Networked Communications

Scaling an engagement organizing model requires a different approach to communications. In the broadcast era, "campaign communications" largely meant getting stories on TV, on radio, or in newspapers. Activities were designed to be media-genic. Communications training was all about how to talk to journalists to give them what they wanted. A joke in political circles said that instead of GOTV meaning "get out the vote," it actually meant "get on TV." But digital evolution is dramatically altering the media landscape as people's orientation to information changes, as we move toward a networked society, and as traditional media outlets face intense competition for attention and advertising dollars from new media. In this new environment, organizations and campaigns need a new definition of what communication entails and new ways of going about it.

Giving up entirely on traditional media is a mistake. The broadcast era is giving way to something new, but established media companies are still hugely influential, particularly as they themselves adapt to digital channels. We campaign in what some call a "hybrid" media environment in which traditional and digital media blend together.[9] Much online content is first produced by traditional media outlets and explicitly packaged for digital platforms. People who cut their cable TV often watch television companies' content online. News stories integrate online comments into their content and sometimes produce stories about issues that break online or even stories about online reactions to stories. Digital outlets hire reporters to join traditional press pools. Bloggers get accredited to cover events. Legacy and new media are truly intermixed.

Although there are now many ways to participate in making and distributing news, it is still true that the top TV stations or newspapers probably still reach more people than anyone else on a consistent basis and are taken more seriously by decision makers. Good campaigns won't see digital and traditional media as either/or but both/and. In the metaphor of information as a stream that we are in together, "power in the hybrid media system is exercised by those who are successfully able to create, tap, or steer information flows in ways that suit their goals and in ways that modify, enable, or disable others' agency across and between a range of older and newer media settings."[10]

In this hybrid media environment, establishing relationships with reporters and designing media-genic campaigns are still important. This is particularly true when campaigns want the air of legitimacy conferred when independent actors such as reporters believe that their activities are worth covering. Getting on TV or in the newspaper increases the perception that campaigns or issues are worthy of attention. Campaigns with resources can still use paid advertising in traditional outlets as a tool to attain this legitimacy and to reach new people.

While campaigns maintain some focus on traditional media, how do they engage with digital media? Another mistake is to see digital media simply as an extension of traditional media, as just another channel to "get the message out." This ignores the different logic of digital media, chiefly that it is a switch from *talking at* supporters to *talking with* them. Mass communications are largely indiscriminate in terms of audience, with few expectations or avenues for feedback. Digital communications allow for personalized interactions in which there is an increasing expectation of interactivity. And, critically, digital communications allow for not only two-way interactions *with* supporters, but also *between* supporters themselves across their own networks without the direct involvement of campaign staff. The ability to scale comes from the ability to harness networks of communications and even networks of networks if a group or campaign joins with other groups or campaigns to communicate together.

The implications for campaigns are profound. When people can talk back, a campaign must not only have the capacity to receive and acknowledge them respectfully but also be open to truly hearing what they are saying and to engage in meaningful dialogue with them. Not only can doing so draw in new supporters or deepen engagement, but also it can bring to the surface new issues to tackle or improve positioning on existing issues. And, if a campaign solicits feedback but is deaf to it, then word will quickly spread that the invitation wasn't authentic, and support will drop off. Truly listening can be a hard step for a campaign to take since it means a loss of control. A few people can't simply decide on a message and let everyone else know what it is. Rather, a jumping-off point can be defined, and a conversation can be established. This is not to say that anything goes or that the conversation moves on to something entirely unrelated. A critical point is that the campaign needs to steward the theory of change in a manner that invites meaningful participation while maintaining focus on achieving its broad goals. Supporters who aren't helping to act on its theory of change aren't really supporters.

A campaign begins to scale when its supporters themselves own and carry its communications goals, adapting and spreading messages across *their* networks. This rarely "just happens" – campaigns need to be designed intentionally to achieve it. Here rigidity around wording or a strong organizational brand gets in the way because people won't participate unless they can make the message their own as a form of personal expression. "Campaigns which give supporters an active role and freedom to customize generate a lot more commitment and enthusiasm and often gain precious insights and innovations by tapping into the collective intelligence of their crowd."[11] Personal storytelling is a powerful way for supporters to plug in – why am I supporting this cause? In networked communications, these stories can be seeded, collected, and held up to inspire others to tell their own stories. A powerful example was the Tumblr feed "we are the 99 percent" that showcased pictures of people holding personalized signs in support of the Occupy movement.[12] Campaign materials can be created to be customized by supporters who want to spread them further. Messages can be crafted and people can be encouraged to adapt them as needed. If they stray from the theory of change, then feedback can be given to check whether a supporter is still on board, and if many drop off then the theory of change might need to be revisited.

Digital tools provide a great means to demonstrate "social proof" that a campaign is worth joining. In the broadcast era, campaigns were at the mercy of media outlets to confer a perception of popularity through their coverage. Today a campaign can design digital communications that publicly show increasing numbers of supporters opting in, which studies show prompts more opting in as others deem it popular and viable.[13] And social tools provide the opportunity for a person to tell his or her network that a cause is worth supporting. In the summer of 2014, tens of thousands of people in Canada, Britain, and the United States participated in the "Ice Bucket Challenge" to raise money for charity by pouring buckets of cold water over themselves, filming it, and posting it on social media while challenging friends to follow suit. The campaign went viral and ended up raising US$220 million for ALS research.[14]

In a more mature campaign or organization with an established snowflake of teams, those teams will develop their own communication desires and needs. The teams will be more powerful when they can tell their own stories to inspire others and tap into their own networks. A campaign can facilitate such storytelling through the provision of information, materials, and a platform. In larger organizations, there is the risk of bottlenecks emerging should these functions not be resourced properly. Ideally, teams will be given the independence to undertake their communications (by having automatic access to digital platforms) without the need for many interventions by a campaign's core team. In sum, networked communications not only use the Internet in the hybrid media environment but also empower supporters to own, adapt, and promulgate the message outside direct managerial relationships of the campaign.

Case Studies

Scaling up campaigns with digital tools, flexible organizing structures, and networked communications has a history of only about a dozen years. US presidential campaigns continue to break new ground in this regard, given their advantages of huge resources and focused attention. Other types of campaigns, though, have adapted those lessons to other contexts. Here I explore the case studies of some recent US presidential campaigns together with the Dogwood Initiative.

US Presidential Campaigns: Labs for Scaling and Networked Communications

In one sense, it is unfair to include US presidential campaigns as case studies since they are unlike anything else in the world. The amounts of money spent are staggering, in the hundreds of millions of dollars. Primary candidates are essentially start-up operations who build an entire campaign from scratch and either win their party's nomination or disappear. The campaigns also command automatic and widespread attention as proving grounds for the most powerful person in the world. This combination of factors creates the conditions for trying new things with lots of money behind them, many of which will fail but some of which can be instructive. Although other types of campaigns will never have as much money or as much focused attention, practices and tools pioneered during US presidential campaigns can be adapted to campaigns everywhere.

Here I look at four campaigns spanning 2004–16, a particularly rich period given the emergence of digital tools and organizing at scale that upended traditional campaigns. Howard Dean set the stage in 2004. He lost the primary but opened people's eyes to what was possible, and in the process he helped to forge new tools and new expertise that carried forward. Barack Obama directly benefited from Dean's run and married sophisticated digital and data practices with the largest grassroots organizing campaign in history – twice. Finally, like Dean, Bernie Sanders did not win, but he broke new ground with a highly decentralized digital-driven campaign and large amounts of money raised via social media. All four campaigns have things to teach us about scaling and networked communications. These case studies are not about the policy positions of the candidates or about Obama's performance in office but about the campaigns waged to seek voters' support.

The Howard Dean Campaign

Howard Dean's 2004 campaign manager Joe Trippi likened it to "plowing snow." By the time of Dean's primary run, companies such as Amazon and eBay had plowed enough snow to get people used to doing things online that a campaign could come along and use the Internet to get big, fast.[15] The Dean campaign would continue to plow snow, clearing the path for other political campaigns. Other campaigns had used the Internet as another broadcast channel with brochure-type websites for people to view and to donate, but Dean would be the first candidate to put the Internet at the centre of his campaign strategy and to treat his supporters as core participants in the campaign.

Although Trippi came from a tech background, the major motivation for an Internet-first strategy was Dean's lack of resources. John Kerry and John Edwards were the party favourites, and Dean was a little-known governor from the small state of Vermont. But his opposition to the Iraq War made him popular among frustrated grassroots Democrats who thought that the party had sold out on the issue. Several blogs independent of Dean began supporting his candidacy and then funnelled money and volunteers to his campaign when he ran.[16] In the days before social media, the comment threads of blogs were places where like-minded people could connect with each other and debate various issues. These bloggers also promoted use of the online service Meetup to schedule gatherings for Dean supporters. Meetup can be used by affinity groups of all kinds to find like-minded people who wish to gather. Trippi recognized the value of the platform and supported its use. Dean supporters quickly outnumbered the other candidates' supporters registered on Meetup, and Trippi set his sights on passing other big user groups, such as the one for people interested in Wicca, which proved to be a tough competitor. "Maybe they were recruiting new witches. Or maybe they could magically create *new witches* when we got too close," Trippi wrote.[17] By the end of the campaign, though, Dean had more – 190,000 of his supporters were on Meetup.

Dean began to translate this grassroots support into fundraising. Early in 2003, Kerry and Edwards were out-fundraising Dean, but by mid-year he had started to catch up. The advocacy group MoveOn held a primary vote among its supporters to see which candidate they supported, and Dean won handily. In the July 2003 fundraising disclosures, he came first in fundraising and then began to emerge as the perceived front-runner. Since no candidate received more than 50 percent in MoveOn's primary, it did not endorse anyone and offered help to all of the candidates. Only Dean took it up on the offer, so MoveOn went to Vermont to coach campaign staff on email fundraising and helped to establish digital best practices for campaigns still used today.

Starting with few resources, the Dean campaign needed to work hard to improve its systems and practices. The campaign began by sending emails through a Microsoft Outlook program on the receptionist's computer, which doubled as the office server.[18] The campaign signed a deal with a commercial provider for database, email, and donation tools. A campaign blog, Blog for America, was started both to communicate on issues and to help set expectations and priorities with supporters in terms of what the campaign needed. The blog was open to comments and quickly became the centre of gravity for the campaign. In communication practices, staff were told to avoid the use of phrases such as "we need your help" or anything that implied a distinction between "us" and "them"; instead, it was "your campaign." The public slogan was "you have the power." The team made it possible to develop a personalized fundraising page off the campaign's website to be able to share with friends. Volunteers developed "DeanSpace," an online tool for supporters to launch websites, manage mailing lists, find one another, and share news and information. The name was a tip of the hat to the early social networking site Myspace.

Staff also began to get a firmer handle on the use of outside tools. The challenge with using Meetup or Yahoo! groups to coordinate local activities is that the data weren't automatically available to the campaign. The campaign tried to manage Meetup groups by asking for data on participants and by developing meeting agendas and setting expectations. It also developed its own application called Get Local, which supporters could use to coordinate their own activities, from which it automatically harvested data. Trippi didn't do away with Meetup, though, since he liked the fact that journalists could see supporter numbers publicly displayed there as a form of social proof to help with legitimacy.[19]

Dean would go on to raise record amounts of money for the time from an email list that hit 650,000 supporters. The campaign once used the occasion of a $2,000-a-plate fundraising dinner hosted by rival Dick Cheney to feature a picture of Dean eating a simple turkey sandwich and asking for support. Dean raised $400,000, double that of Cheney.[20] But donations could come from anywhere in the United States, whereas Dean needed to have an impact particularly in the early primary voting states of Iowa and New Hampshire. As a front-runner, he attracted attacks from other candidates that began to eat into his polling numbers in Iowa. Also, the campaign was having a hard time translating the Meetup groups into what it needed in terms of voter contact. A better job was done in New Hampshire, where campaign field organizers managed the Meetups themselves and gave volunteers what was needed for voter contact. There state director Karen Hicks was trained by Marshall Ganz and adopted the house meeting tactics of Fred Ross and the United Farm Workers union to build a coordinated field campaign.[21] This was one of the seeds of the Obama approach, and Hicks went on to play a major role there. Iowa, though, had no such effort, and there was an ill-advised last-ditch effort to parachute in thousands of Dean volunteers from elsewhere.

For a variety of reasons, Dean came third in Iowa and second in New Hampshire, and his momentum was gone. After losing a few more states, he dropped out of the contest. The legacy of the campaign, though, lived on. The campaign turned over its email list to a new group called Democracy for America, which continues to recruit, train, and fundraise for like-minded candidates. Dean himself went on to become chairman of the Democratic National Committee and set to work modernizing the party infrastructure. He brought together messy, state-level voter lists into one national list, and he commissioned an interface to the list called the Voter Activation Network, or VAN, still used by Democratic campaigns. Dean staffers also carried forward what they had learned. Some founded the firm Blue State Digital, which developed integrated campaign software for use among progressive campaign groups and it would be used by Obama. Others founded the New Organizing Institute to train a new generation of campaign staff in both digital and field campaign best practices. When Obama ran in 2008, he had the Dean campaign to thank for plowing the snow and developing tools and practices that would help him get to the Oval Office.

The Barack Obama Campaigns

Regardless of what people think of Barack Obama as president, the campaigns that earned him the White House will be studied for years to come. In contrast to the freewheeling Dean campaign, the Obama campaigns were meticulously planned and rigorously executed. They embraced a culture of measurement and testing and applied it relentlessly to all activities. In contrast to the Dean campaign, the Obama campaigns were much clearer about what they needed from volunteers and built it into their tools. At the same time, the campaigns set a tone of empowerment, with the slogan "Yes We Can."

The 2008 Obama campaign assigned every voter in the country a pair of scores based upon the probability of showing up to vote and supporting Obama. These scores were built using multiple data points, including past voting history, commercial data, and surveys, and they were used to create algorithms to predict behaviour based upon shared patterns.[22] These scores were used to guide canvasses and phone banks, with their results fed back into the campaign to refine the data models. The use of predictive analysis for each voter is like a "virtual ID," in contrast to a "hard ID," which comes from direct contact with a person. The latter is prohibitively expensive to do for every voter.[23]

The campaign launched My.BarackObama.com (MyBO) on the Blue State Digital platform that let supporters schedule their own events, launch personalized fundraising applications, write blogs, and network with one another. As with DeanSpace, the name was a tip of the hat to Myspace. In the early days of the campaign, the attitude was "don't wait for us; don't wait for somebody to tell you what to do," but as time went on staffers reached out to leaders on MyBO to set expectations and goals.[24] By the end of the campaign, 2 million people had created profiles on MyBO, 200,000 events had been scheduled, 400,000 blog posts had been written, and 70,000 people had created their own fundraising pages that had raised $30 million.[25] The campaign also worked with Blue State Digital to develop Neighbor-to-Neighbor, an online calling tool integrated with the voter file, which empowered volunteers to do things that staffers used to do, such as enter data.[26] The campaign blog was used to collect and highlight the stories of volunteers working on the campaign and thus set a tone of collective empowerment.[27] By the end of the campaign, it had collected 13 million emails. Overall, the tools had furthered the campaign's goal of creating "a customized, highly productive individual relationship with every person in the country."[28]

With regard to measurement and testing, the campaign later estimated that optimization of its activities to make them more efficient or effective was worth $57 million, enough to pay for its overall operations in Florida and Ohio.[29] The campaign knew to the penny, for example, how much it cost to get a new email and how much it was worth for fundraising. It tested various splash pages on its homepage and boosted email signup by 40 percent.[30] Facebook was in its early days of penetration, but still an important organizing tool, particularly on campuses. Over 2 million people liked Obama on Facebook, and the campaign developed apps to encourage friends of his fans to volunteer or vote in target areas, to register to vote, and to find polling places.[31]

But the hype about Obama's digital data work can create the perception that geeks in the basement press a few buttons and a campaign is won. Notes one close observer: "Future campaigns that hope to model themselves on [Obama for America] by becoming a 'high-tech political start-up' at the expense of their people operation will find themselves with accurate lists of voters and nobody to do the work of speaking with them."[32] The other story of the Obama campaigns is about how they recruited, trained, and structured a massive body of volunteers in probably the most sophisticated field operations in history. It was the 2008 Obama campaign that popularized the snowflake model in campaign circles everywhere.

There was huge excitement about candidate Obama, with tens of thousands of people signing up online to volunteer. The 2008 campaign trained 3,000 organizers to help 1.5 million people play active roles in local leadership teams across the country.[33] It helped that in 2008 the Democratic Party machine was backing competitor Hillary Clinton, so the Obama campaign couldn't rely on existing party infrastructure and was forced to build something better.[34] The campaign slogan for volunteers was "Respect. Empower. Include." In the early days, paid campaign field staffers were challenged to meet targets for volunteer and leader recruitment rather than voter contact. This is a nerve-wracking switch since it leaves a campaign behind target for voter contact in the first few months, relying on greater numbers at the tail end as the volunteer teams kick in. But, as Obama battleground states director

Mitch Stewart points out, "if you have folks that invest early in the volunteers, you start a bit slower, but the growth that you see in the end is explosive and much more so than what you could do if you had just staff-based activity."[35]

This is how the campaign built its snowflakes. A new volunteer would sign up through the Obama website and get a call from a field organizer to do a one-on-one meeting. They would discuss the volunteer's values and skills, and the organizer would make a request that the volunteer take on a specific task. This was also a test. If the volunteer delivered, she or he would be asked at subsequent one-on-one meetings to undertake bigger activities, such as organizing an event or leading voter contact. Eventually, the volunteer could be asked to take on a team leader role with a title, complete with a binder laying out the job description in writing. The volunteer team had prescribed turf and was responsible for voter contact in that area. The team leader had periodic meetings with the paid organizer to report on progress toward targets and to be coached through any challenges. A team had captains responsible for functions such as canvassing, phone banking, volunteer managing, and data organizing.

The campaign supported fieldwork with specialized access to voter data by volunteer team leaders, traditionally the purview of paid staff. Volunteers who signed up were automatically segmented by geography and sent right away to field organizers as prospects for follow-up. Volunteer leaders designed and led canvass outings and were trained to provide space for debriefing afterward. In this way, teams formed meaningful social bonds that kept people engaged. Each paid field staffer oversaw several volunteer teams and was in turn held accountable and coached by a paid regional field staffer, thereby adding tiers to the snowflake. Training took place all the time at the individual level and at weekend-style longer training sessions called Camp Obama, co-designed by Ganz.[36] Participants learned how to do one-on-one meetings, recruit for house meetings, and lead volunteer teams. They also learned to use personal narrative to motivate activity, telling the story of "self, us, now," just like Obama did on the campaign trail.

At the end of the campaign, Obama won with 53 percent of the popular vote and 365 electoral votes. Not only did he win, but also his campaign found that good organizing is personally transformational. One Obama neighbourhood team leader named Jennifer said that

I'm a different person than I was six weeks ago. Now, I'm really asking: how can I be most effective in my community? I've realized that these things I've been doing as a volunteer organizer – well, I'm really good at them, I have a passion for this. I want to continue to find ways to actively make this place, my community, a better place.[37]

The 2012 Obama re-election campaign repeated everything from 2008, only more intensely. In 2012, campaign organizers knew that they had to get those who had voted for Obama in 2008 to vote for him again and had to register and mobilize new voters to compensate for any past Obama voters who would stay home or had defected to the other side.[38] For data, the campaign built a system that it called Narwhal to synchronize in real time users' various interactions with the campaign, which had been siloed in 2008. This allowed it to have a complete picture of any one person and to optimize interactions with supporters based upon their past activities.[39] For targeting, it added two more scores based upon the likelihood of being persuaded to turn out to vote and of supporting Obama,[40] following the work of social scientists who ran experiments on responses to different messages.[41] For example, variations on a flyer were sent to a target area in a randomized manner, and then follow-up calls were made to test its impact, broken out by demographics. The campaign expanded its analytics department to fifty-four people to assist other departments such as fundraising and communications.[42] The 2012 Obama analytics were so good that by the day of the election their county-level predictions were within tenths of a percentage point of actual results.[43]

The campaign designed an interface called Dashboard for its supporters, with more of a drive to have people sign up for local teams. Supporters could still launch personal fundraising pages, form groups, and post their own updates to local groups or to the national news feed. In 2012, the campaign gathered 30 million emails, almost half of its eventual vote of 65 million. Facebook was a bigger network than it had been in 2008. Obama racked up 32 million likes on Facebook, thirteen times more than in 2008.[44] The campaign developed a targeted sharing app on Facebook that could determine which of a supporter's friends it needed to reach and reached out to that supporter to ask her or him to follow up personally. Some 600,000 supporters contacted 3.5 million targeted voters in battleground states.[45] Digital director Teddy Goff described the Facebook tool as "the most significant new addition to the voter contact arsenal that's come around in years, since the phone call."[46]

The 2012 campaign reprised its snowflake structure for fieldwork. Even after four years of governing had tempered enthusiasm, the second Obama campaign still engaged 2.2 million volunteers through 10,000 teams,[47] and 4,000 paid field organizers supported this effort. The campaign set up a national training department, the first presidential campaign to do so.[48] Three of five team leaders and one of five team members put in over ten hours a week.[49] In 2012, the campaign also let well-trained volunteers play larger roles in making persuasion phone calls, informed by experiments that showed this approach to be effective.[50] On the last day of the campaign alone, more than 100,000 canvassers knocked on more than 7 million doors, and twice as many volunteers worked the phones.[51] Obama won with 51 percent of the popular vote and 332 electoral votes.

The Bernie Sanders Campaign

In some ways, the Bernie Sanders primary campaign was a rebellion not just against the careful, structured nature of the Obama campaign but also against the traditions of organizing itself. "Organizers began to develop this expectation that organizing should be incredibly difficult," says Zack Exley, one of the architects of the Sanders campaign and a veteran of both MoveOn and the Dean campaign.[52] He believes that many supporters are already leaders and don't need to be tested and trained before being given responsibilities. To be sure, as with the Dean campaign, necessity played a role in the Sanders campaign, which embraced a highly distributed, volunteer-driven voter contact program. Sanders started with little money and was up against Hillary Clinton, perceived as having a lock on the nomination. Nevertheless, the message from Sanders resonated with the grassroots, and by 2016 digital tools and social media had advanced to the degree that it was possible to quickly motivate and shape a nationwide groundswell into a coherent campaign. The trick was to strike a balance between throwing open the doors to volunteers to run the show and providing enough structure to win. "We've seen the limitations of a model that says if you just get a whole lot of people to do something – you just flood the streets," says Exley. "Without actually building an organization that can provide leadership, what do you get after you topple Mubarak?"[53]

Co-architect Becky Bond calls the resulting approach "Big Organizing." She notes that the media focused heavily on the data elements of the Obama campaign and that "Big Data is about narrowing down the possibilities and minimizing the work necessary to meet goals at the lowest cost. So, in some ways Big Data is about the small campaign. In a Big Organizing model where volunteers manage and grow the volunteer base, we're building the big campaign."[54] And build it they did, relying on digital tools to an unprecedented degree. It helped to have a candidate who hadn't changed for decades, boosting his authenticity. Sanders is a self-described democratic socialist and about as far from a packaged candidate as it gets. His message of a system rigged in favour of the wealthy struck a chord with thousands (as it did for ultimate election victor Trump).

Sanders began modestly, announcing his run to a few journalists outside the Senate. In the first twenty-four hours, he raised a million dollars online. His digital team asked for it all to be invested in online fundraising ads but instead got $250,000. This paid off, with millions coming back quickly.[55] Scott Goodstein worked on Obama's digital team and then helped to run the social media campaign for Sanders, and he noted that, while the Obama campaign kept digital operations quite siloed, "the Bernie Sanders campaign has let the digital team be baked into the entire DNA structure of the campaign."[56] The Sanders campaign recruited volunteers online and asked people to step up to host meetings at which Sanders would speak via live stream to communicate what was needed. Event hosts received an organizing guide and materials. More committed volunteers were called "builders" and given extra training via the phone or online. The intention was for teams to form to undertake the mechanics of voter outreach.

While the campaign devoted more resources and paid organizers to the states that voted earlier in the primary calendar, Exley and Bond were given responsibility for helping the later ones. They went about filling as many campaign roles as possible with volunteers. They developed a "barnstorming" model in which a supporter was asked to book a venue, and then the campaign would email and text other supporters in the vicinity inviting them to show up in person for an organizing meeting. At that meeting, people would commit to hosting voter contact events and right away recruit others in the room to attend them rather than wait until later to follow up. In this model, there was little ladder of engagement for supporters or testing of volunteers, since people were plugged in right away. Said Exley: "If you ask me, the most innovative thing to talk about here is the way we're setting volunteers up to make commitments to each other instead of to paid staff, in ways that ensure follow-through on hard, scary things like hosting phone banks and leading canvasses – and all the tools and techniques that allow for all this to scale massively."[57]

The campaign made innovative use of digital tools. To comply with the law, for volunteer phone banking, it developed a system dubbed the "Bernie Dialer" to manually line up calls to people on cellphones and merged it seamlessly with people called on their land lines by an auto-dialer. In this way, volunteer callers were simply presented with people to talk to and could therefore have many more conversations using web-based calling software.[58] Phone banking was used to harness volunteers around the country to call into target states to identify supporters so that the volunteers in those states could focus on turning those supporters out to the polls. Half a million supporters signed up, dialing a total of a million people a day at its height. The digital director said that "it's possible we've developed the largest capacity for voter contact in history."[59]

The Sanders campaign also made wide use of existing apps. It used Slack, an online collaboration tool that lets teams come together and communicate in real time without emails or texts, using a smartphone or a home computer. And, if challenges come up, a Slack user can tag a knowledgeable volunteer or staff member for follow-up. Facebook was widely used, with hundreds of pages and groups set up independently or by the campaign. It used an app called Hustle to send and track text messages among volunteers, staffers, and potential supporters. For example, within sixteen hours, texting helped to secure 235 attendees at an event when thousands of hours had been logged using other means to get just 465 commitments.[60] Said Goodstein: "Campaigning has always been about three variables. It's always been about time, people, and money. These social media tools we're leveraging have made it easier for us to spend less time organizing more people, and for less money."[61] A volunteer programmer created an online map on which every Sanders canvass, phone bank, or campaign event around the country was visible. It became heavily populated, social proof to potential new volunteers that there was momentum, and it encouraged them to plug into an existing event or to create their own.

Volunteers came up with the successful Twitter hashtag #FeelTheBern. The campaign adopted it, which provided a signal to artists and others that the campaign was open to their contributions. In March 2016 in Portland, a bird landed on the podium during a speech by Sanders, much to the delight of those in attendance. The campaign immediately edited a video of the moment and pushed it out to 2 million Twitter followers. Graphics of "Birdie Sanders" were developed with wispy white hair like Sanders himself. Via email and Facebook, people were asked to donate to receive stickers, and $3.6 million was raised in a few days. Said Trippi, Dean's campaign manager, of the bird moment: "If that had happened in 2004, there is not a damn thing we could have done. Now, you have the prowess to take advantage of it and the network that they built on, and you can do amazing things with it."[62] The campaign would go on to raise $230 million, with $216 million coming online and $114 million via email, and 43 percent came from mobile devices.[63]

All things weren't smooth, though. Exley points to the "tyranny of the annoying," the principle that for every group of 100 people, there will be one so disruptive that the group is turned off from participating, especially when "the worst people with the most time on their hands take over."[64] He advocates that Slack groups not be more than thirty people to safeguard against this, and he wants more tools for moderating the group and designating its leader.[65]

Sanders mounted an unexpectedly strong campaign but came up short. He might well have caught Clinton had he started earlier, and as the Democratic nominee he might have achieved a different result in the general election that followed given the nation's anti-establishment mood. A worthwhile debate centres on the relative merits of a more decentralized approach in which volunteers do more overall but perhaps to less exacting standards. Exley and Bond seem to rely on redundancy in "post-scarcity" organizing in which a campaign can conceivably knock on every door and call every voter – the equivalent to flooding the field. Says Bond: "In Big Organizing, scale is limited only by the appeal of your ideas and not the number of staff the campaign can deploy."[66] Nevertheless, in the spring of 2016, the Sanders campaign did have more staff than the Clinton campaign, 865 to 765,[67] so it wasn't all just volunteer power.

The Donald Trump Campaign

The election of Donald Trump as US president in 2016 came as a shock not only to those who care about progressive values but also to campaign professionals. His opponent, Hillary Clinton, deployed many of the tactics of the Obama campaigns and outspent Trump significantly. Trump, meanwhile, disparaged the use of data and invested little in field organizing. But his disturbingly hateful campaign dominated the media and successfully tapped into many Americans' desire for change, while Clinton was perceived as representing the status quo and failed to motivate progressive voters to turn out in the right places to win an Electoral College victory. The lesson is that message can still overwhelm mechanics, and campaigns ignore that at their peril.

Although all four campaigns described here pulled in volunteers at scale and used networked communications, they were ultimately transactional campaigns that let supporters decide how to support the candidate's election but not to determine the candidate's policy positions. Distributed volunteer leadership did not extend into policy influence, but this might also be a question of timing – electoral campaigns are equivalent to sprints to the finish line, and they are less appropriate for that kind of conversation. In Chapter 6, I will return to the question of whether political parties can truly be movements in which supporters have such influence. Nevertheless, US presidential campaigns continue to be laboratories for learning about how to scale with the help of digital tools, networked communications, and flexible organizing structures. Each one draws in hundreds of thousands of participants, who then go on to work on other campaigns and apply what they have learned, thereby enriching the practice of campaigning itself.

Dogwood Initiative, Part 2: Riding the Engagement Cycle

Every other year the Dogwood Initiative publishes a report on its failures. It does so to reinforce a culture of risk taking and learning. Everybody fails at times, but few talk about failure openly and use it as an opportunity to become stronger. In the earlier Dogwood case study, I dove into the weeds of its tech systems to show how they evolved to support the organizing and growth of Dogwood. Here I explore how Dogwood has gone through several cycles of engagement, sometimes failing along the way but turning that failure into learning and ultimately into success, including standing up to the most powerful industry on the planet.

Will Horter once almost shut the doors of the Dogwood Initiative forever.[68] A lawyer by training, he cut his campaign teeth in the anti-apartheid movement and was hired to lead Dogwood when its mandate was forest policy reform. The early days of Dogwood involved "flitting" among issues and writing reports. Many advocacy groups survive on funding from philanthropic foundations, but Horter was finding it hard to land enough grants to keep staff employed. He considered packing it in.

Instead, he took a chance. It was 2006, and the oil pipeline company Enbridge was threatening to build a pipeline from Alberta to the northern BC coast. Horter suspected that increased oil tanker traffic on the coast would be a visceral issue for British Columbians, and federal Minister of Natural Resources Gary Lunn's riding was close to Dogwood's office. Despite having no funding to support it, Dogwood decided to hit the streets with a petition. The response was overwhelming. Two students hired to work street corners in Lunn's riding were mobbed by signers. Dogwood began its first real push to align and mobilize people at scale.

Lunn was a minister in a minority federal Conservative government subject to checks and balances by other parties. When Horter asked the Leader of the Opposition Stéphane Dion to stand against tankers on British Columbia's northern coast, he replied that the issue needed to expand to the rest of Canada to be taken seriously by his party. Horter was wondering how to do this with little money when he partnered with Rethink Communications, a progressive public relations firm in Vancouver. It worked with Dogwood for free to come up with an ingenious concept: a decal that would adhere to dollar coins, covering the loon that appears on one side to appear as if it was in an oil spill, with the campaign URL appearing below it. Dogwood had tens of thousands of these decals made and asked supporters to stick them to coins for circulation.

The URL led to an online map for people to put a digital pin where they found a "No Tankers" coin and to tell their own stories. Within forty-eight hours, someone had found one across the country in Halifax, and within weeks the map had filled up. "It made people feel powerful," said Horter. The government was ignoring them, but here was social proof that they were many and connected. Horter realized that people hunger to be part of something bigger than themselves. The Canadian Mint threatened Dogwood over defacing currency, adding to the publicity (the Mint ultimately backed down). The opposition party came onside, and the issue started to gain traction in the buildup to the 2008 federal election. It was time for issue realignment and a new mobilization.

Lunn had a battle in his riding, but his opposition was split three ways. Dogwood began to work there, encouraging citizens to vote for a candidate who would commit to limiting oil tankers on the BC coast. Only Lunn refused. Dogwood canvassed, staged events, and leafletted the riding. Lunn squeaked out a win, but his government was once again held to minority status. Dogwood learned that what it was doing wasn't enough to have a large impact. It had to go both bigger and deeper, developing more and deeper relationships – building more power.

The new federal opposition leader Michael Ignatieff distanced himself from everything that his defeated predecessor had done, so again Dogwood had work to do. It canvassed for petition signatures in the riding of a key opposition caucus member who had won by a razor-thin margin. It also set up a robocall to the list of donors to the opposition party, recorded by a former member and minister who had championed a ban on tankers. The new opposition leader came onside. This set up a clear differentiation for the next federal election, held in 2011. Dogwood chose a different race in the Victoria region to work in and again encouraged citizens to vote for an anti-tanker candidate. Again only the Conservative candidate refused to take that position. This time Dogwood fielded a team of thirty-five volunteers and staff who canvassed, called, and staged events. The Conservative candidate lost by 406 votes.

Although Dogwood felt better about its election work this time, its people were exhausted, and they had worked in only one place. Worse, despite a loss in this riding, the Conservatives achieved a majority and would now pursue an aggressive pro-tanker agenda. How could Dogwood scale up its efforts and have a meaningful impact beyond just one place? It couldn't rely on a staff-driven model. Up to that point, Dogwood had been engaging its network only in issue alignment and mobilization. The answer to going bigger would lie in distributed leadership, in getting to true engagement organizing.

Celine Trojand started her political education in the bucket of a tractor on her farm in northeastern British Columbia, listening to her mom talk about issues with visitors.[69] Later she taught English overseas and worked in retail, and she was intrigued when Dogwood posted a position for an outreach coordinator. She applied and got the job. She was uncomfortable calling herself an "activist" and settled on "organizer" instead. Trojand worked through the 2011 election for Dogwood and was learning on the job. She realized that there was just too much work for one person and started delegating it to volunteers. But she still didn't have a way of talking about it or scaling it up.

The new Conservative majority government would help. It came out aggressively promoting oil projects and dispatched its minister of natural resources to label critics "radicals." It also gutted environmental laws, muzzled government scientists, and audited environmental charities. Dogwood had set a target to recruit 30,000 new supporters in 2012. After the attack on "radicals," Dogwood signed up 31,000 people online in just three weeks. The Conservative government was creating the perfect conditions for organizing. Trojand believes that people come together in greater numbers when the power deficit goes from being uncomfortable to being intolerable. "Organizing is the antidote to the feeling of powerlessness, uncertainty, and unsettledness," she says.

The potential to scale was there, but Dogwood failed to achieve it. It put new supporter recruitment on hold while it tried to figure out how to plug in the people who had already signed up. It developed a "Find Leaders" kit to outline how supporters could self-organize, but it got bogged down in trying to make it perfect. Several months were lost in planning. The new contacts went cold.

In the spring of 2013, the Leading Change Network went to Vancouver to do a Ganz-style training session for organizers. Trojand attended it and found a way of talking about what she was trying to do. As she told her peers, "I'm not making this stuff up!" Dogwood needed a theory of change that would build an organizing snowflake. The National Energy Board (NEB) was holding hearings on the Enbridge pipeline proposal. Thousands of people signed up to oppose it, but Dogwood knew that the NEB would ultimately rubber-stamp the proposal. Unlike in other provinces, however, voters in British Columbia have recourse to a citizens' initiative process in which provincial legislation can be proposed and voted on by citizens themselves.

The bar is high for gathering signatures but it had been met once before in a fight over tax reform.

Dogwood began to think about a citizens' initiative to deny Enbridge the provincial permits that it would need. It was a compelling theory of change and would require building teams across British Columbia. The idea caught on. Trojand travelled the province turning the energy against Enbridge into a snowflake structure of teams. Each team had a leader and captains for things such as gathering data, canvassing, and even enjoying "culture" – responsible for fun. The teams mobilized by going door to door with petitions, thereby building a base of supporters in anticipation of a citizens' initiative that would require an intense process of signature gathering over a short period. At its height, there were about 120 teams in over forty provincial ridings. Moved by growing public and First Nations opposition, the BC government issued five conditions that it wanted satisfied before agreeing to the project. This requirement, along with First Nations lawsuits and over 100 conditions imposed on Enbridge by the NEB, effectively stalled the project. Dogwood had helped British Columbia to stand up to the biggest industry on the planet and win, without actually running the citizens' initiative but building the credible threat of one. Now it needed another issue realignment.

The 2014 Vancouver municipal election had a tanker angle to it given Kinder Morgan's proposal to twin its existing pipeline into the area and increase tanker traffic there. The incumbent mayor and council had taken a strong position against the proposal, again setting up a clear contrast to other candidates. Dogwood's teams mobilized with a calling program to boost voter turnout among existing supporters in Vancouver. In British Columbia, the public can view the municipal voters list after the election to see who voted, and Dogwood staff spent hours in Vancouver City Hall looking at these records. It found that Dogwood supporters who had received a phone call were 20 percent more likely to show up at the polls. The success of this program convinced Dogwood to plan for a much larger phone mobilization for the federal election in 2015.

Based upon past elections, about a dozen federal ridings in British Columbia appeared to be close races between pro- and anti-tanker candidates. Dogwood teams focused on calls to those ridings to turn out other Dogwood supporters to vote but not telling them how to vote. Instead, Dogwood commissioned a series of riding-level polls so that voters could see which way the political winds were blowing in their areas. Teams began cold-calling people in the phone book to increase the number of supporters and then shifted to GOTV calls. The latter asked voters about their plans for voting, in line with behavioural research showing that people are more likely to go to the polls if they can visualize the logistics of doing so. To provide social proof to volunteers, each day Dogwood emailed participating callers the total number of calls made and told stories about the conversations. When the dust settled, Dogwood had made 42,541 calls in addition to sending over 200,000 emails and 18,000 texts. Without a publicly available federal voters list in Canada, it is hard to measure causality, but voter turnout was 2 percent higher in ridings where Dogwood worked, over and above the national spike in voter turnout. The pro-tanker Conservatives lost all but two ridings touching tidewater.

Each time it has journeyed through the engagement cycle, Dogwood has gained more supporters, volunteers, and donors than it has lost, and it has grown in the process to become a regional powerhouse. What's next for Dogwood? Both success and failure have taught it lessons, and it takes them seriously. Both Horter and Trojand have identified the need to keep decentralizing systems and networking communications to give local teams more autonomy to do their work and to tell their stories without things getting bottlenecked at head office. Says Trojand: "If the campaign doesn't have a compelling story, and if people aren't hearing it, then you aren't going anywhere. I don't think you can take a campaign to scale doing engagement organizing if you don't have people who are thinking about how to tell your collective story and how to reach different audiences."

Horter also sees the need to set a higher bar for admission into a position of responsibility in a Dogwood team, even for a volunteer. Such a person needs to have a feeling for what the organization is starting to call "Dogwoodiness." For Horter, "it's really about your relationship with power." Issues will come and go, but what remains constant is building citizen power, and the organization will be more selective in working with people who buy into that. "We'll grow slower, but there'll be less turnover," says Horter. "We'll see it if works. It's all a big experiment."

Lessons for Engagement Organizing

When campaigns marry the organizing practices explored in Chapter 1 with the new digital realities explored in Chapter 2, they can quickly scale up, but doing so will require attention to an engagement cycle, to structuring volunteer leadership in an appropriate manner, and to networked communications. As these elements come together, a group or campaign is in the zone of engagement organizing. Here are the lessons from this chapter:

- *Plan for an engagement cycle.* Engagement organizing goes through overlapping phases of issue (re)alignment, mobilization, and distributed leadership. Repeating the cycle can grow the campaign or organization.
- *Align and realign issues.* Be open to grassroots energy and facilitate alignment or realignment of a critical mass of people around issues to move to action.
- *Mobilize.* Help to design higher-effort activities to advance the issue within a shared theory of change, and help to identify leaders along the way.
- *Distribute leadership.* Consider a snowflake structure to form interlocking teams of organizers, leaders, and volunteers who hold one another accountable for meeting campaign goals.
- *Network communications.* Shift from "speaking at" supporters to "speaking with" them, and foster their ability to own and carry campaign communications across their own networks – "speaking between." Meanwhile, work with both traditional and digital media outlets in the hybrid media environment.

chapter 4

Disruption in the NGO Sector

The more we can create structures where regular people can plug in,
connect to each other, and stand up for what matters, the more
possible it will be to transform the deepest injustices in our society.

– Nicole Carty, SumOfUs

Compared with other entities such as unions and political parties, NGOs have the fewest structural rules governing their behaviour. People can come together informally and start acting like an NGO, but many go on to incorporate so that they legally exist and can do things such as get bank accounts. Beyond not making a profit, what they decide to do and how they decide to do it are largely up to them. Some NGOs might decide to seek charitable status so that they can give tax receipts to donors, in which case more rules will apply. But charities, too, can practise engagement organizing since the resulting activities do not need to be political. Even some churches employ certain engagement organizing principles to develop new members.[1]

This freedom means that NGOs are often the first to try new things, and this seems to be the case with the advent of engagement organizing. NGOs have been some of the first adopters of it in Canada and therefore have a lot to teach others. These first adopters are often growing quickly and increasingly setting the public agenda. At the same time, only a minority of

Canadian NGOs are practising engagement organizing. In this chapter, I explore some of the reasons for this disconnect before turning to case studies of Leadnow and Ecology Ottawa, two NGOs that are leaders in engagement organizing today.

Disruption versus Inertia

There are thousands of NGOs operating in Canada today, working on everything from Indigenous justice, to delivering meals to the needy, to debating economic policy. Most are modest in size, and almost none has a guaranteed income flow, so there is great fluidity and turnover in the sector, with groups constantly being born and folding. We have already explored larger historical trends for NGOs and other entities, such as the arrival of the broadcast era, which aided a transition after the 1960s from more participatory service organizations to more professional single-issue groups staffed by experts and reliant on direct mail fundraising. In Canada, this was coupled with government funding in the NGO sector, a mixed blessing given that the groups delivered enhanced programming for a while but became vulnerable to the cuts that came with a change in regime.

Today NGOs are subject to the same disruptions and opportunities sparked by the erosion of the broadcast era and the rise of a new digital landscape. Just as media outlets are undergoing a profound restructuring, so too established NGOs now find themselves in an environment in which their relevance is being challenged by new NGOs that use digital tools and practices to effectively compete for support or even by citizens starting their own campaigns online. Open Media, SumOfUs, and Avaaz didn't exist ten years ago and can now directly reach over 2 million Canadians. The Dogwood Initiative once struggled for attention among BC NGOs, but now it competes very effectively with a quarter of a million supporters. By the end of 2014, NGO newcomer 350.org had helped to organize thirty campaigns for fossil fuel divestment on Canadian university campuses. Leadnow and Ecology Ottawa, dealt with in the case studies below, are likewise relatively new organizations that increasingly set the agendas in their respective constituencies. And any of these groups could be eclipsed by new start-ups five years from now. Older organizations are still doing good work but must now compete for energy in the NGO ecosystem with nimbler newcomers

that have lower overhead and the ability to bypass the media to rally supporters directly.[2]

This shifting of public attention brings challenges to legacy groups' rev-
enues as supporters, donors, and foundations see other groups setting the
agendas. This gets at the heart of the NGO "business model." Digital tools
are starting to displace direct mail as a staple for fundraising. A Canadian
study found that, though older donors still respond well to direct mail,
"Generations Y and X are far more likely to give online, and as many Baby
Boomers say they give online as via direct mail." Interestingly, the same study
found that Generation Y is "more likely to demand accountability and transparency than older donors."[3] Groups that forge direct ties with citizens
through digital tools are at an advantage over those that prospect for donors
among the public. Organizations such as Dogwood have had good results
by turning online supporters into monthly and one-time donors by using
the phone to make requests. There is therefore value in achieving scale in a
supporter base, which new groups are doing well digitally. Foundations are
also attracted to a group with a large supporter base since they perceive an
ability to reach large numbers of people and make an impact.

Established groups are adapting. Most have a digital presence, and the
larger ones have entire digital departments devoted to building their social
media presence and pursuing digital fundraising. Whether they can keep
pace with the lower-overhead issue generalists remains to be seen, particularly if the Internet is used simply as another channel to *talk at* supporters
about the group's work instead of using it to *talk with* supporters and engage
them to carry the mission. This requires a certain letting go of the organizational brand and an openness to bringing supporters into the mission in an
authentic way, which requires making more fundamental changes than just
adding digital tools.

Standing in the way of sectoral disruption is inertia. In theory, NGOs
have only a few legal requirements and are therefore free to change how
they do things in response to threats and opportunities. In practice, organizations develop systems, practices, and cultures that are hard to change. An
empirical observation is that engagement organizing has emerged with
groups that are either new or have gone through a crisis that forced them to
let go of established patterns. Organizational inertia comes in several forms.

Here I explore four of them: staff, systems, culture, and governance. It is necessary to understand this inertia to be able to better overcome it.

Many current NGO staff came of age during the broadcast era, when the accepted model of social change centred on hiring experts who had little interaction with supporters. Media staffers were prized for their ability to package messages and their relationships with journalists, and lobbyists were valued for their relationships with politicians. Fundraisers were expected to master direct mail, one-on-one major donor requests, and proposal writing. Anybody technical was called "the IT guy" (and it was almost always a guy) and put in the basement. Today a group that wants to shift toward engagement organizing might find itself with a staff with these kinds of skills and aptitudes unsuited to the new model. A limited budget implies the need to replace staff members, but many NGOs are slow to move them out of unsuitable roles, even though this tardiness can hobble both the goals of NGOs and the careers of employees. Staffing an engagement organizing model requires gregarious organizers who spend most of their time out of the office, tech people who play a central role in developing organizing strategies and the tools to execute them, communication specialists who help *supporters* to communicate and not just the organization, and fundraisers who embrace many channels to raise money. A group will also do better when its staff complement reflects the makeup of the constituency that it is helping to organize, based upon gender, race, age, and other factors.

Systems inertia begins with an organization's software and extends to its practices. Engagement organizing is about developing relationships, and if an organization has more than about 200 of them then it needs a system to track and nurture them in the right ways. As Ecology Ottawa's Graham Saul asks about his work, "how can we have a meaningful conversation with 20,000 people?"[4] Legacy organizations are often saddled with multiple systems that don't talk to one another, and as new needs arise more disconnected systems are added. This creates headaches as data are manually transferred between systems or as supporters are treated differently by different departments. An organization serious about engagement organizing will invest in systems that track and activate supporters at scale and in a unified manner. This can involve some pain at the front end as systems are replaced and integrated, but it will pay off in results over time.

Organizational culture is hard to pinpoint but critical to tackle. As management guru Peter Drucker famously said, "culture eats strategy for breakfast." Culture is comprised of the values, behaviours, assumptions, and attitudes of staff and key volunteers that help to determine things such as motivation and whether initiatives succeed or fail. A group's culture is like its personality. It builds over time and is difficult to change. An organization that wants to shift toward engagement organizing will face cultural inertia – a tendency to do things "the way they have always been done." The shift to an organizing culture is a big one since it asks us to stop being the experts and acting on others' behalf and instead to start focusing on stepping into the background and encouraging others to act for themselves. If staff and key volunteers aren't fully bought in and excited by this new direction, then they will sabotage its execution either intentionally or passively. This means that staff, key volunteers, and supporters need to be brought into a conversation about why the organization is making the shift and how it will help to fulfill its mission. Those not excited by the opportunity might need to find another group with which to work.

Finally, a shift to engagement organizing can encounter inertia rooted in patterns of organizational decision making or governance. Many groups are used to a model in which decisions are made by a small group of board members or an executive team and then communicated to others to execute. An organizing model turns that model on its head. Organizing begins with listening to a potential constituency and acting on what has been heard. Then supporters expect an ongoing conversation about chosen activities and what's next. Volunteer leaders expect a seat at the decision-making table as a condition of their ongoing work. All of this adds up to a letting go of control relative to a traditional model of governance, and those used to making decisions by themselves need to be retrained or encouraged to participate in a different group.

Being conscious of the various forms of inertia can help a group to overcome them. Involving its key people in this conversation is a good way to both identify barriers and earn support for changes. The best way forward, however, is just to start. As Dogwood organizer Celine Trojand says, "we act ourselves into a new way of thinking instead of think ourselves into a new way of acting."[5] Taking on a new engagement organizing campaign begins to build the right muscles and the right thought patterns. Ultimately, inertia in some groups will necessarily give way to the disruption sweeping the sector. Those that don't adapt will face increasing pressure for relevance and financial stability. The NGO landscape has always been fluid and is especially so now during the erosion of the broadcast era and the impacts of that erosion on institutions of all kinds. Dominant groups today look different, act and think differently, from those of ten years ago and will be different again ten years from now.

Embracing Power and Being Leaderful

NGOs are relatively free to chart whatever theory of change they want, and there are many types of change and many paths to get to them. A diversity of groups undertaking different kinds of activities is a good thing. How does engagement organizing fit into these theories of change? The practices described in the first three chapters can be applied to varying degrees by any group that takes seriously the challenge of bringing people into its mission at scale to reach its goals. Whether it does so or not depends in part on how it thinks about power.

As discussed earlier, people have an awkward relationship with power. On one level, it offends our sense of justice that society doesn't work by the rational interplay of ideas. It doesn't seem fair that vested interests with a greater *ability to act* – one definition of power – should prevail. When we talk about "building people power" through engagement organizing, there is an understandable discomfort with the fact that we need to do this in the first place. Talk of things such as "issue alignment" and "mobilization" can sound like a bunch of radicals plotting a revolution.

Yet every NGO needs to be able to act, and without financial endowments most will need to rely on people. For example, Reforest London, an Ontario tree-planting group, set the audacious goal of planting a million trees and knew that it couldn't do so with staff alone.[6] It didn't have sufficient ability to act. So it has been applying engagement organizing principles to draw in volunteers not just to plant trees (a form of mobilization) but also to run teams of other volunteers (a form of distributed leadership). It goes door to door giving out seedlings and encouraging people to become involved. It has an online tree-planting leader board to demonstrate that the initiative is growing and to hold up those leading the charge. It routinely tells the stories of volunteers, describing their motivations and passions. It is using engagement organizing for what most would consider an uncontroversial cause, even though it is enhancing its power. Any organization working with people can integrate elements of engagement organizing into its theory of change, and indeed we can find hospitals with pyramids of engagement and churches with snowflake structures for their congregations. The goals do not need to be political. Registered charities have rules restricting their political activities, but they can apply engagement organizing to their non-political work.

There is another kind of awkwardness in our relationship with power that inhibits engagement organizing. This one is internal and involves the power relationships among those aligning and mobilizing together. Should one participant have a greater ability to act than another? This gets at the issue of leadership and whether it should exist. Some argue that digital tools have reduced the need for structured coordination, and though this is true in some ways others argue that leaderlessness itself is desirable. Why recreate the flawed power structures of broader society within our campaigns? Fully participatory democracy is not only more just but also more engaging. We see this play out during what are called "movement moments," when an uprising gathers steam, such as with Occupy Wall Street, the Maple Spring protests in Quebec, and the First Nations Idle No More movement. Sociologist Zeynep Tufekci studies such movements and concludes that "it is crucially important to note that this particular style of organization – ad hoc, leaderless, participatory, and horizontalist – is often a desire expressed by protesters. Again and again, in interviews in multiple countries and settings, and in the public writings of many protesters, there has been great emphasis placed on the value of participatory organizing that resists formalization and institutionalization."[7]

Setting aside for a moment the question of values around power and leadership, there does appear to be something to the conclusion that movement moments naturally lean toward horizontalism. Uprisings are rarely well planned and draw in so many people so quickly that slotting them into anything more than a rudimentary structure is impossible. Leaderlessness lets such people immediately own their participation and vote with their feet to join. The question, though, is how long they vote with their feet to stay.

This is where the ideals of pure democracy run up against the pressures of group dynamics. Any group of people will always develop informal leaders, and many are relieved that they exist, that there will be leadership so that there is a conscious direction and people's time isn't wasted. As one Occupy participant writes, "the mantra of leaderlessness came from a genuine desire to avoid classic pitfalls into hierarchy, but it was, at the same time, a farce, and divorced from any sense of collective structure or care for group culture."[8] Denying the existence of leadership denies an honest conversation about accountability, about making leaders responsible in a transparent fashion. As a result, Occupy denied itself the leadership to evolve beyond its initial tactic even as it became clear that momentum was being lost. In other contexts, leaderlessness might not be as fatal, particularly if the starting point was a simpler "no" to a specific injustice that can be overturned (e.g., the Maple Spring) or to an unpopular figure who can be turfed.

For those seeking to learn more about Idle No More, it is appropriate to listen to First Nations voices themselves, such as those gathered in *The Winter We Danced*.[9] When the movement plateaued, Indigenous scholar Gerald Taiaiake Alfred advocated the reoccupation of Indigenous sacred, ceremonial, and cultural sites led by traditional chiefs and clan mothers, medicine people, elders, and youth "to present more of a serious challenge on the ground to force the federal government to engage our movement and to respond to us in a serious way."[10] Embedded therein is a call for a form of issue realignment, mobilization, and distributed leadership.

Leaderless movement moments have shown their ability to harness "stop" energy, but they struggle with creating "go" energy.[11] Without distributed leadership, the ability to adapt a theory of change to changing circumstances is diminished, and there are fewer opportunities to form and maintain solid relationships in team settings. This breaks the cycle of engagement as a campaign falters and people move on to other things. By burning brightly for a while, however, movement moments can change public opinion and give rise to new initiatives. The Occupy movement successfully put income inequality on the public radar, where it was picked up in various ways by politicians, from Barack Obama's 2012 campaign to Justin Trudeau's 2015 run. Idle No More set the stage in Canada for the release of the Truth and Reconciliation Commission report, the recommendations of which were endorsed by the Canadian government. The Indignados movement moment in Spain sparked a major new political party.

Others see a role for leadership in movement moments, albeit a redefined one. Rather than being leaderless, movements can be *leaderful*.[12] This can be defined in various ways but sees leadership coming from many places in a campaign simultaneously. Leadership isn't hoarded but intentionally shared and distributed. Moreover, leaders see their role as helping others to step up and not just to do the job themselves. Oprah Winfrey waded into this debate recently when she said that she was looking for leadership in the Black Lives Matter movement similar to that seen in the civil rights era. Those involved took offence, with one responding thus on Twitter: "So does @Oprah expect someone to raise their hand at Protest when they ask 'who is your leader'? That messiah style of leadership is not us."[13] Another replied that, "If @oprah doesn't see 'leadership' in Ferguson, it's cuz she's not really looking. It's grass-roots – she has to do work to see the teams."[14] Each movement needs to wrestle with the balance of creating structured and distributed leadership and the need to empower supporters to chart their own paths. Engagement organizing seeks that balance.

Case Studies

There are thousands of NGOs in Canada working toward a better world and making change with a diversity of theories of change. A whole range of groups is needed to fill all the niches, and it would take many books to describe even half of them. I have chosen Leadnow and Ecology Ottawa for case studies here since they are two groups practising engagement organizing that are part of a wave of newer organizations bringing disruption to the NGO sector. These groups didn't even exist ten years ago, yet today they are increasingly out-competing established organizations for attention and influence.

Leadnow: Next Generation Organizing
A friend took Logan McIntosh along to an environmental meeting on the University of Alberta campus, where she was a student.[15] Intimidated by her first experience with this kind of gathering, McIntosh sat in the corner and tried to understand it all. She barely heard snippets such as "Tarzan was growing super fast and destroying everything." After a while, she figured out

that they were saying "tar sands." Eight years later she was running one of the largest independent field campaigns in the history of Canadian elections for a new organization called Leadnow, an advocacy group working on progressive issues across the country.[16]

Leadnow was born out of frustration that the Canadian political system does not reflect the popular will of voters. An antiquated voting system gives false majorities in Parliament and as such does not reflect citizens' desires on issues such as climate change. Co-founder Jamie Biggar saw the impact that MoveOn had in US politics and wanted to bring the model to Canada.[17] In 2008, during a minority federal government, Biggar helped to create Canadians for a Progressive Coalition, a website and petition asking Canada's opposition parties to work together. Elder statesmen Jean Chrétien and Ed Broadbent gave the campaign a boost by carrying the same message, but collaboration wasn't to be. Still, Biggar ended up with a list of over 5,000 names that would become the seed list for Leadnow.

For systems, Leadnow contracted with a company called Engaging Networks, which has an integrated online tool for petitions, emails, and fundraising. Early on, Leadnow worked to get supporters to develop relationships with one another in person. In 2011, it ran a process called Regeneration, which consisted of eighty house parties across the country to come up with a cross-party agenda for Parliament. This began the practice of bridging from online to offline and bringing people together in person at key moments.

In the election that followed, Leadnow helped to encourage "vote mobs," high-energy events by university students to encourage youth voting. Campuses competed to make it onto Leadnow's online map of vote mobs as a form of social proof showing people that they were participating in something bigger than themselves. The bad news for Leadnow was that a hostile Conservative Party won a majority government. The good news for Leadnow, though unknown at the time, was that this majority government built the organization by providing a foil to motivate supporters and around which to organize.

Leadnow started a pattern of rapid responses to hot-button issues for progressive Canadians, sending online petitions to its list, asking signers to share with their social networks, and staging creative events. During this phase, Leadnow's engagement cycle was only getting to mobilization rather than to distributed leadership, but it was growing along the way. For example, the Conservatives proposed a new crime bill to expand police powers and increase mandatory minimum sentences. Leadnow responded with a petition and mobilized a day of action with 100 events outside the offices of members of Parliament, with the theme of "Don't Mess Up like Texas," after conservative Texans decried their state's own expensive practice of filling up jails. An amended law did pass, but some parts were later struck down by the Supreme Court of Canada. Importantly, Leadnow added another 30,000 names to its list.

Leadnow repeated the days-of-action tactic on different issues. Supporters would be asked online if they were willing to host rallies; if they were, then they would be given support materials and a list of local names to contact and they would be trusted to talk to the local media. Says Biggar: "If you meet people where they are at when they care the most, people are willing to be active. It's amazing how a not very political person will go from signing a petition to hosting a rally. It's because we ask." During this rapid-response phase, Leadnow's online list grew to hundreds of thousands of Canadians. The organization then turned its attention to preparing for the 2015 federal election and the need to build a real ground game, which meant getting beyond mobilization to distributed leadership.

Leadnow's young staff had lots of enthusiasm and talent but no training in organizing. Offline actions were one-off events, and volunteer leaders weren't consistently nurtured or formed into teams. McIntosh was now onboard and knew that Leadnow needed to get to the next phase. At this point, Leadnow and other groups adapted the work of the Leading Change Network and Ganz to Canada. The task of building out Leadnow's first snowflake began. Organizer Jolan Bailey piloted the method in an area of Vancouver that Leadnow knew would be a battleground in 2015. He started with a list of people who had come out for past Leadnow canvassing in the provincial election and built a team with captain roles for gathering data, canvassing, and undertaking community outreach. The roles were provisional in anticipation of a strategy still being finalized.

How Leadnow decides on priorities and strategies is instructive. It has a small board and a relatively flat staff structure, and it practises deep listening with its supporters. It surveys its extensive e-list regularly with questions about priorities and positions, and it sometimes conducts in-person deliberative events, such as its Regeneration series. Its core volunteers are engaged in developing and testing new messages and websites. Its teams make many tactical decisions on how to implement what the wider Leadnow supporter base has decided. There are critics of this type of consultative model, in which final decisions are still made by a few people, but McIntosh says that, "if it were truly a few people making the call, it wouldn't work that well. We win by engaging lots of people. For us we're finding we build better campaigns if we're informed by what people want to do."

Bailey's Vancouver team began to work together and became skilled at door knocking with a survey asking about issues and political preferences. It also helped to mobilize for a climate day of action, which the team found strayed too far from its election-focused theory of change, and for a petition on voter suppression, which the team found was a good fit. In the spring of 2015, Leadnow hosted events called Connect, at which supporters were asked to come out in person to workshop its election strategy. These events not only provided valuable feedback but also served to recruit more people into teams. Leadnow had a ladder of engagement running from those who said online that they were "hand raisers" or potential volunteers, to those coming out for events, passing some leadership tests, and being asked (in a one-on-one meeting) to take on a team role.

The strategy took aim at vote splitting in Canada's first-past-the-post election system. In 2011, the Conservative Party won a majority of seats in Parliament with only 39 percent of the vote because the rest was split three and sometimes four ways. In 2015, Leadnow therefore encouraged citizens to vote together for the candidates best able to defeat the Conservatives in selected races predicted to be close. In a post-election debriefing, it spelled out its theory of change like this: "If enough of people in Conservative swing ridings united behind the best local candidate who could defeat the Conservatives, we could stop the riding-by-riding vote splitting that twisted a minority of votes into a majority of seats for the Harper Conservatives."[18] Its intention was to do this for one election and then to press for electoral reform so that it would not need to do it again. The organization would commission polling to determine the best alternative candidate and back up its choice with canvassing, phone calling, and doing online work.

Bailey's team in Vancouver swelled and then split into two. Bailey stepped out of the team leader role as others stepped up to fill it. Importantly, the teams now had good clarity on a theory of change and a tactic directly on point – a petition asking whether voters would consider voting together to defeat the local Conservative candidate. Canvassing increased to a couple of outings per week per team. Leadnow added NationBuilder to its data systems. It needed to use the functionality for field campaign organizing, giving team leaders specialized access to their teams and recruitment prospects as well as generating canvass walk lists or phone bank lists. Each team had at least one data captain responsible for one or more volunteers who helped the team to use NationBuilder.

As the election got closer, Leadnow applied the lessons that it was learning in Vancouver to scale up into other ridings across the country. It hired riding organizers for each of its tier one priority ridings and regional organizers for bundles of its tier two priority ridings. These organizers set up at least one team per priority riding, shaping existing Leadnow volunteers into more structured team roles and getting them moving on riding outreach with a "Vote Together" petition. Leadnow put into place campaign infrastructure on the expectation that, once people turned their attention to the election, more volunteers would come. As McIntosh now says, "the hockey stick is real." There was a slow build of volunteer participation and suddenly a spike, making a graph of it look like a hockey stick.

For an independent actor in an election in Canada, the stats are impressive.[19] Leadnow recruited 5,626 volunteers to make 51,617 targeted voter contacts either on the phone or on the doorstep. It had forty-five local teams in its snowflake and more intensely supported those in targeted ridings. Without a publicly available voters list in Canada, it is hard to measure Leadnow's impact, but voter turnout was from 5 to 10 percent higher in ridings where Leadnow worked, and the Conservative candidates were defeated in twenty-six of the twenty-nine ridings targeted. Another reason that it is hard to measure impact is that the 2015 federal election saw a surge in support for the opposition Liberal Party in the final days, as voters tired of the incumbent government consolidated the "change" vote in one party. Such big shifts tend to overwhelm the impact of fieldwork, though you can't predict that. Leadnow played a key role in shaping the larger media narrative in the campaign toward strategic voting to defeat the Conservatives, which helped to give permission to the larger electorate for the surge.

Leadnow's strategy worked best in two-way races in which the choice of best competitor to the Conservative candidate was clear. In Canada's multi-party system, however, three- or four-way races are common – and more complicated. Leadnow's most controversial call during the election was in the Vancouver-Granville riding, which turned into a three-way race. Leadnow decided to make a candidate recommendation there even though polling showed the Conservative running third, negating the need to endorse another candidate. But, as per the plan, Leadnow put the decision to a vote of its community, and its internal vote selected the New Democratic Party (NDP) candidate. The Liberal candidate went on to victory, again showing the limitations of an outside campaign during an election surge. At the time, the organization felt the pull of its volunteers, who had invested huge amounts of time, and wanted to follow through on the plan. In hindsight, Leadnow staff would have had an honest conversation with their supporters and been clear on why they would not be able to run an endorsement process.

In a debriefing with teams after the election, Leadnow was pleasantly surprised with the desire of volunteers to keep going – to restart the engagement cycle. Volunteers liked the discipline of well-organized teams with a solid theory of change, clear roles, and well-defined targets. This contrasts with other NGO volunteer opportunities, which often have none of those things. A key challenge for Leadnow moving forward is balancing its online rapid-response mobilizing work with its face-to-face organizing work. It shares some DNA with digital organizations such as SumOfUs that don't invest in the latter and therefore have more resources to devote to the former. When organizing is viewed as a choice, it can be viewed as expensive, with the need to hire organizers to do the slower work of having conversations. Ultimately, it comes down to a group's theory of change and whether the group believes that it can achieve its mission without engaging people offline.

Ecology Ottawa: Going Deep in One Place
In 2011, Mayor of Ottawa Jim Wilson walked into Ecology Ottawa's annual banquet, expecting perhaps fifty people.[20] Instead, there were about 250. He was amazed that a local environmental group had so many supporters. By 2015, the same banquet had about 600 people, including elected officials from both the provincial government and the federal government. Ecology Ottawa built this influence through engagement organizing. It's a good example of using the model on a more local scale.

Graham Saul did things backward compared with many advocates.[21] He began working on social change internationally, spending time with Oxfam in Africa before returning to Canada to coordinate national climate advocacy. By 2007, though, he had become convinced that the best way to make change was at the local level, and he helped to found Ecology Ottawa. From its first days, Ecology Ottawa knew that it needed a volunteer-driven model. It didn't have the resources to hire enough staff to get to scale, and his experience working at the national level convinced Saul that elected decision makers would move only if their own constituents were pressing them to move:

> At the end of the day, we always felt that the only way to make change is if people in the politicians' wards – their voters – are demanding it. The difference between us as a group of people with an opinion as opposed to a group of their voters with an opinion is huge. Our overarching philosophy is how to get people engaged in demanding change.

The group therefore set out to find people in Ottawa who cared about the environment and to connect them to issues and decision makers. An early example of issue alignment was a petition on sewage. To this day, Ottawa dumps raw sewage into the Ottawa River. Ecology Ottawa began a petition to fix this problem because it was so obviously wrong. It was an easy issue around which to align people. The petition was pushed out online, at events, and on doorsteps. People who sign petitions are followed up to receive newsletters, to volunteer, and to donate. Doing so not only advances the issues but also builds the organization.

This is a good example of an issue that fits Ecology Ottawa's criteria for selection. The organization selects binary issues (you know if you've won or lost), which are simple to understand, emotive, and impactful. All campaigns are designed to provide opportunities for volunteers to join and provide leadership. Depending on what a person fills out in an online volunteer form, she or he might get a phone call from a person working on data, communications, or an issue campaign. Sometimes during big mobilizations, such as GOTV work or big events, Ecology Ottawa will run a volunteer phone bank and turn people out for it. The group is careful to track all data. Like Dogwood and Leadnow, it uses the NationBuilder data system, which automatically logs all interactions that people have with the group's online communications. During a recent speakers' event to which 1,300 people came, each attendee had to pass through a phalanx of volunteers to sign in, with information then logged into the database.

Ecology Ottawa uses a pyramid of engagement with five levels, from basic contact information at the bottom to somebody taking on a distributed leadership task at the top. Saul says, however, that they sometimes see it as more of a mountain range than a pyramid: "We may have somebody at the top of the donor pyramid or the Facebook pyramid, so we may need to interact with them differently." As an aspirational goal, Ecology Ottawa also wants to get better at communicating with people on their preferred interests, since it has this information via various online tools, but as a smaller group it finds it harder to have the bandwidth for extensive segmentation. As a city-based organization with a lot of participation on multiple issues, Ecology Ottawa finds it harder to maintain a neat and tidy snowflake structure. Some people come into the organization based upon a single issue, while others are content to work geographically in their neighbourhoods, and some activities involve both. The group therefore continually reinvents its teams based upon circumstances. During an all-hands-on-deck mobilization such as an election, a tidier snowflake might emerge temporarily, but after it more messiness ensues.

In terms of governance, Ecology Ottawa pulls together team leaders and strong contributors of time once or twice a year to debrief and discuss strategy. A smaller steering committee of the same type of people meets more regularly and charts the day-to-day operations of the organization. A legal board is composed of three steering committee members and is responsible for fiduciary duties. The board never discusses anything that hasn't first gone to the steering committee.

As Ecology Ottawa has grown, its relationships with local politicians have matured. Elected officials now know that the group can turn out voters and other groups at key moments, and sometimes they ask for this to happen. Saul sees the group's role as creating the space for elected and unelected officials who want to do the right thing to move forward. Politicians have learned that they will earn kudos for doing good things and get called out for doing bad things. Often it's a matter of not letting something drop off the city government's list, as happens frequently. Ecology Ottawa played an instrumental role in getting the city to follow through on its climate change plan, even in the face of a hostile environment committee chair (the group succeeded in getting a better chair). The group helped to get a budgetary increase to fund the goal of planting a million trees. Ottawa's complete streets strategy, in which multiple uses are prioritized and not just cars, is now one of the best in North America.

Ecology Ottawa has chosen a path that's difficult but gets results. It's not always easy to stay the course. As Saul reflects, "there's something genuinely a lot easier in approaching the work in other ways, in not organizing. That's not necessarily more impactful, though. It's not always intuitive to people that this is the best way to make change. We have to constantly resist the impulse to sit behind the computer screen writing reports and sending email to each other."

The City of Ottawa has a ward system in which its elected officials represent a part of the city rather than being elected by voters citywide. A few years into its work, Ecology Ottawa realized that it was quickly gaining supporters downtown but fewer in the suburbs. Saul realized that it could create a winning coalition on council only by building power in the suburbs. In 2013, Ecology Ottawa focused both its fundraising and its petition canvassing in Orléans, a suburb of Ottawa where it had virtually no presence. It knocked on about 43,000 doors and recruited about 1,000 new donors, with even more signing a petition. Follow-up included both online activities and invitations to in-person events. Orléans became a core part of the Ecology Ottawa universe, alongside downtown areas, influencing city councillors in that region.

Gillian Walker is an example of an Ecology Ottawa team leader.[22] She grew up in Ottawa but wasn't very active then. She went to university in Victoria, where she would sit on the beach and worry about oil spills. "It would have been me going down to the beach to clean up oil off the rocks, and I didn't want to do that, so I started organizing instead," she said. She became a team leader with the Dogwood Initiative after going through training. When she returned home, she realized that Ecology Ottawa was using a similar model of engagement organizing and participated in door knocking for the 2015 federal election.

After the election, an Ecology Ottawa staffer took Walker for lunch to do a one-on-one meeting. She was "escalated" in her responsibilities to take on a team leader role, anchoring the Ottawa Centre team that happened to be in the riding of the new federal environment minister. After the election, the team was feeling its way toward new roles. It started organizing a community meeting with the minister and soliciting community leader participation. Walker needed to start doing her own one-on-one meetings with team members but found that the culture wasn't there yet. "People avoid them a bit. The other day I reached out to a team member to go for coffee and said we are also planning a team meeting. She said she will try to make the meeting and totally avoided the coffee. You can't give them an easy out." So she started to build the routine of one-on-one meetings to make them normal.

Ecology Ottawa puts a good deal of effort into training in three ways. It partners with other organizations to run periodic weekend training sessions using the Ganz syllabus. It runs periodic Saturday training sessions on the craft of organizing. And, during the summer when its ranks swell with students, it has lunchtime training sessions on various dimensions of organizing. A real challenge is finding leaders for the various tiers of its snowflake. As Ecology Ottawa gets bigger, Saul finds it harder to find volunteers to help lead volunteers who themselves are leading volunteers – the third tier of the snowflake. It takes a level of emotional complexity to take on tasks similar to managing staff while keeping people motivated, particularly during times when campaigns are less mechanical, such as during elections. "Leadership development is the ultimate challenge," Saul says.

Lessons for Engagement Organizing

NGOs are diverse and have many different theories of change. The erosion of the broadcast era is bringing disruption to the sector in the form of a new campaign landscape for NGOs and the appearance of new digital-first groups that compete for relevance and support by leveraging the reach, speed, and cost effectiveness of digital media. Engagement organizing is one response to this new environment that takes advantage of the ability to engage more people more quickly at scale to advance a goal. Here are some lessons for NGOs:

- *Be aware of how the NGO sector is facing disruption and adapt.* A new generation of nimble, digital-first NGOs is emerging to compete for relevance and support. Organizations that want to thrive today must understand how to be like them.

- *Uncover sources of group inertia and overcome them.* Your staff, your systems, your organizational culture, and your governance can all be sources of inertia preventing a shift to engagement organizing. Identify and address these sources consciously.

- *Incorporate engagement organizing into your theory of change.* Any group working with people at scale can benefit from applying engagement organizing practices. Become comfortable with the concept of building power, and embrace distributed leadership.

chapter 5

Rediscovering Union Organizing

A union is not simply getting enough workers to stage a strike.
A union is building a group with a spirit and an existence
all its own ... built around the idea that people must do things
by themselves, in order to help themselves.

– Cesar Chavez

My friend Karen looks at me across the table in the coffee shop and says, "the labour movement is in trouble, and everybody knows it. We're tinkering around the edges, but we're not finding a way to really engage our members." She has just retired from working in Canadian union leadership for nearly three decades. Then she adds, "we got into the habit of doing things for our members instead of helping members do things for themselves. And, if they're not in the habit of taking on the battle themselves, they're not in the habit of taking on a battle at all."

We come full circle in engagement organizing to find the circle broken. As we saw in Chapter 1, Saul Alinsky was inspired by the industrial unionism of the 1930s and carried the lessons that he saw there into community organizing. But today, with some exceptions, we see less organizing happening within unions to engage their existing members or to recruit new ones. The percentage of unionization is dropping, with only 15 percent of Canadians working in the private sector belonging to a union in 2014.[1] And the participation of existing members in the inner workings of their unions is anemic.[2]

The challenges facing unions are well documented. One recent book even shouts in its title *Canadian Labour in Crisis*.[3] Labour leaders give speeches about the need for something different, and occasionally a manifesto for change is debated at a union convention,[4] but, as Karen puts it, "it's often rah rah, but it's not do do." To be fair, as we saw in the previous chapter about NGOs, change is hard even for small organizations with few legal constraints. Unions are much larger entities and therefore have a good deal more inertia to overcome. And the legal structures that govern them are complex and provide the wrong incentives to good organizing.

Although change is hard to achieve, it's not impossible. The shifts in the economy to more mobile capital, smaller workplaces, and more precarious service sector jobs are major external challenges for unions. At the same time, there are factors within union control that can be tackled more readily. Indeed, being strong enough for the external challenges requires overcoming the internal ones. Unions in Canada have over 4.5 million members, a huge potential source of strength. In terms of organizations of people in Canada, labour is a sleeping giant and really the only giant. The case studies in this chapter include UNITE HERE Local 75, a union that maintains a strong organizing culture, and the BC Government and Service Employees Union (BCGEU), pioneering digital and data innovation to improve organizing. First, though, it is useful to recap some of the core challenges facing unions to see what must be overcome.

The Postwar Servicing Model

The framework that defines unions today emerged around the time of the Second World War. Until then, unions engaged in strikes to achieve recognition and were often confronted with aggressive, and sometimes violent, responses by both companies and governments. The plus side was that this environment forced unions to constantly engage workers in collective mobilizations to achieve their goals. This was the era when songs such as "Solidarity Forever" were written. In the mid-1930s in the United States, the New Deal and the Wagner Act brought new rights to workers there. Canadian workers were often members of international unions, so expectations grew for similar legislation in Canada. Labour shortages and strikes during the Second World War, together with political competition on the left, pressed Prime Minister William Lyon Mackenzie King to pass Order in Council P.C. 1003 in 1944, which established compulsory collective bargaining. If a union could prove to a labour relations board that it had majority support in a workplace, then it became legally certified, and the employer had to negotiate with it in good faith. Unfair labour practices could be ruled on by the board.

In 1946, Justice Ivan Rand arbitrated an end to a strike at a Ford plant in Windsor and established what is known as "dues check off." Workers in a certified workplace were not required to join a union, but they were required to pay union dues because all workers benefited from the union's activity. The employer collected these dues and submitted them to the union. Rights and responsibilities were further codified in Canada in the 1948 federal Industrial Relations and Disputes Investigations Act. Provincial governments followed suit with their own legislation. Unions finally had a basis to achieve recognition, some predictability around bargaining, and a path to financial stability. At the same time, their ability to strike was highly regulated. A key part of this framework was the "grievance" system. With a contract in place, a process was established to settle disputes (or grievances). In the past, a disagreement might have been settled by mobilizing workers to demand change. Now steps were laid out whereby a worker would file a claim alleging that the contract had been violated, and this claim would get taken further up the chain of command by union and management officials and if necessary by lawyers in arbitration. The process could take years.

The overall framework set the stage for tremendous gains for unionized workers. In the postwar boom, unions bargained for ever higher wages and benefits. The rate of unionization also continued to climb, particularly with the addition of public sector workers. But cracks started to appear in the 1970s. A recession shifted the political consensus, and governments began to roll back union rights and to use back-to-work legislation more frequently. Meanwhile, globalization picked up steam, offshoring manufacturing jobs and creating a service economy less conducive to unionization. After 1984, Canada's level of unionization began to fall, while at the bargaining table unions were pressed for concessions. Rather than organizing new workers, some unions merged to retain their membership levels. People started talking about the "crisis" in labour.

Today various aspects of this sixty-year-old framework present challenges. An obvious one is that it was created to serve an economy in which large, stable workplaces were common. Unions developed tactics to unionize these kinds of employers and relied on the resulting dues to pay for these campaigns. Today, though, two-thirds of private sector employees are in workplaces with fewer than 100 employees.[5] By some estimates, unionizing one worker now costs $1,000,[6] and if true then this imposes a disincentive for a union to go after smaller, lower-salary workplaces, where it would take a long time (if ever) to recoup this cost via union dues.

Aside from costs, there are legal barriers to union certification and reaching a collective agreement that are harder to overcome in smaller workplaces with lower salaries and more transient workforces.[7] Franchises present the challenge of determining the correct bargaining unit to unionize, since an employer might own more than one location. Even if a union organizer can figure out who all the full-time and part-time staff are to sign union cards, the battle is still not over, since legally speaking there is no union without a first contract. An employer must negotiate in good faith but is under no obligation to compromise. If a strike results, then the hardship to an employer of a relatively small workplace shutting down is also relatively small, and the incentive for lower-income workers to stick with the battle is likewise small. A resulting contract might therefore simply reflect the status quo, and with no upside to paying union dues a decertification follows, and the union disappears.

Another challenge is that the grievance system conflicts with the "iron rule" of organizing: *never do for others what they can do for themselves*. Instead, postwar union organizing became defined narrowly as achieving a collective agreement in a new workplace, and then things shifted to servicing members under that agreement, in which union officials performed tasks on behalf of members. For example, *The Steward Handbook* of the Canadian Labour Congress for 2015 points out that union stewards are often the only points of contact with members, but casts the role as distinct from that of a union organizer, to "represent" the department by serving the members.[8] Many labour analysts point out that a servicing model makes members disengaged and passive.[9] One says that "members have often become so accustomed to staffers doing the bulk of union work that they expect staff to do this – after all, some members say, 'that is why they are paid so much money.'"[10]

The dues check off system has helped to create an environment in which unions have fallen behind on using technology and data to build power. When the employer rather than the union collects dues and data on employees, unions are in a subservient relationship regarding information on their own members. At least one Canadian union only recently embarked on building its first database of members. Most Canadian unions have incomplete member data, or data scattered across several places, sometimes jealously guarded by union locals that don't share them with union headquarters. After its 2015 federal election push, in which it actively reached out to members to encourage them to vote, Unifor had about 55 percent of its members contactable in a central database and thought that it was doing better than many other unions.[11]

With unions feeling that they are under siege, they might be tempted to adopt a defensive posture to hold onto what they've got rather than embracing change. Union officials and stewards might just be trying to keep their heads above water and have little capacity to do much else. If labour is to move beyond crisis, though, things will need to change – and change significantly. Overall, unions need "to consider more carefully what in the post-war model of labour relations is worth defending, what needs to be transcended, and what never really worked to create power for workers in the first place."[12]

Rediscovering Organizing

The starting place for a newly powerful labour movement is the rediscovery of a broader definition of organizing. Unions helped to create modern organizing and need to reclaim it. If labour organizing continues to be narrowly defined as achieving new certifications and collective agreements for selected groups of workers, and then servicing them instead of empowering them, then unions will continue to face disengagement by existing members and remain irrelevant to most of today's workforce. To fix this, labour organizing can return to its roots and reclaim its tradition of building power with workers of all kinds to help them help themselves. There are three categories of workers to organize: those with an existing collective agreement, those with a potential collective agreement, and those for whom a collective agreement might not be possible. Part of the shift in thinking is that workers in each of the three categories can be considered union members and that organizing with each of them is an ongoing process of empowering workers to act together; it's never over. (For an example of one union's more robust organizing principles, see the appendix.)

Many of the principles and lessons of engagement organizing can be applied to rejuvenating union organizing, but there are also some traits specific to labour. Particularly, in contrast to an NGO, which attracts a self-selecting group of people based upon commitment to a cause, a workplace consists of a pre-established group of people who have gone there for a job and not necessarily for a union. This affects the approach to the engagement cycle and to distributed leadership. As with any human group, a workplace will inevitably develop "organic" leaders – those people to whom other workers will turn to solve problems or get advice. They might be different from those more pro-union or more outspoken, but they are the ones able to mobilize others. The job of a union organizer is to listen carefully to identify these organic leaders and then to develop them by encouraging them to step up to a more visible leadership role as part of the union. Organic leaders can become stewards or play a leadership role as a member of an organizing committee. In this way, a snowflake structure is built in the workplace with the goal of having each member included in a formal or informal group with an organic leader.

What are organic leaders mobilizing other members to do? The answer is as much as possible, as long as members do things together and develop their own agency. "The experience of collective action changes people, especially (but not only) when the action is successful. It gives workers a sense of their power. It opens people up to ideas about the possibility of making change they previously thought made no sense."[13] The traditional form of collective action in a workplace is the strike, and building a strong leadership structure will give a union a better read on the degree of member support for a strike as well as provide a stronger base for action. Labour organizer Jane McAlevey writes that "strikes are essential to restoring the power of the working class, not just for the better standards strikes can produce, but also because they reveal high-participation organizing."[14] However, if strikes are infrequent, then other collective activity is needed to keep people doing things together and building their power. McAlevey describes her time working in Nevada hospitals in which all members and not just a few representatives were invited to be part of contract bargaining, to come in person and play a role in the process.[15] She also advocates "whole worker organizing" to recognize that workers don't live two separate lives but face challenges outside the workplace too. This involves members in collective mobilization outside the workplace, such as preventing the demolition of an affordable housing project where members live.[16] And union activity in the community helps to establish relationships that can be brought to bear during workplace conflicts.

Ultimately, prioritizing collective rather than individual action and making space for workplace organizing means taking emphasis off the grievance process. Currently, many of labour's resources and much of its bandwidth are used up by a tactic that neither fosters workers building their own power nor coming together with others to do so. In Nevada, McAlevey began to develop a "Fast and Fair" grievance process in which every two weeks a team composed of both workers and managers got together to hold one another accountable to the contract. Despite other significant organizing achievements in Nevada, she considers this to be some of the most radical work done there since it was the start of a new model of unionism in which, "instead of functioning as alienated and powerless labor, nurses were pulling up a seat at the table to actually engage in reforming hospital practices."[17] In another example, in Canada, MoveUP, the western Canada local of the Canadian Office and Professional Employees Union (COPE), is working to handle the beginning stages of grievances closer to the source.[18] By training its stewards better in both labour law and conflict resolution, MoveUP wants to enable union staff to focus on larger, systemic workplace issues. Without backing down on enforcing contracts, unions need to find ways to have the grievance process take up less time and fewer resources so that they can focus on more collective activity led by their members.

As we've seen, a shift toward organizing means a shift in how decisions are made. This can be challenging to many unions that have structures for internal governance that evolved under the servicing model, in which a small executive is elected to run the show regardless of the level of participation by members. But "unions have to create the space for rank and filers to strategize and plan. Democracy can be a hot mess – but there's no shortcut around building leaders who know what they're fighting for."[19] Unions that wish to rediscover organizing might need to investigate new models for decision making and governance.

A renewed focus on organizing and engagement in unions will inevitably bring about advances in digital and data infrastructure, particularly as union leaders who volunteer in political party campaigns wonder why their practices aren't applied to union organizing. Indeed, it has already started to happen. In 2014, United Steelworkers Canada created a Department of New Media and Information Technology, and the BCGEU has something similar. Unifor has started to use NationBuilder for member organizing. The United States is arguably further ahead given its larger scale and proximity to technology and data experts from American presidential campaigns. American Federation of Labor and Congress of Industrial Organizations (AFL-CIO) Deputy Political Director Michael Podhorzer helped to start the Analyst Institute, a body devoted to bringing randomized experimentation to test the effectiveness of engagement tactics.[20] The AFL-CIO also runs regular digital strategy training sessions available online. The United Food and Commercial Workers (UFCW) in the United States uses Facebook extensively to find and recruit workers at Walmart and to help them self-organize through local online groups.[21] There is considerable digital and data expertise in the labour community to draw on as unions catch up to political parties and NGOs in using these tools to organize and build power.

Returning to a broader definition of organizing and embracing a digital and data culture are two things that unions have significant internal control over and can move on right away. But what about the external challenges facing unions? In today's fluid service economy, how can unions reverse the decline in unionization? And how can unions help to build power with workers who might never have a collective agreement? A good start is allocating more resources to organizing new workplaces. Recent data are hard to find, but a 2001 survey found that less than 7 percent of union resources went into organizing new workplaces and that 20 percent of unions spent no money on doing this.[22] There are some signs that this is changing. When Unifor was founded in 2013 by a merger of the Canadian Auto Workers and the Communications, Energy and Paperworkers unions, it made a commitment to spend $10 million a year on new organizing. Canadian locals of the UFCW commit 10 percent of their resources to organizing new workplaces, with the target of doubling membership by 2018.[23] Other unions are also investing in new organizing, including in the service sector, and having success.

To deal with a fragmented economy, creativity is also needed. The Service Employees International Union (SEIU) is running a long-term campaign spanning the United States and Canada to unionize janitors and get better deals for them by going past the janitorial contractors that they officially work for to target the companies that hire these contractors instead. Called "Justice for Janitors," the campaign uses a variety of tactics to bring publicity to the working conditions of janitors and to put responsibility on commercial building owners and the larger brand name companies for which the cleaning is done. The campaign also relies on citywide pressure across employers to establish standard base rates in a geographic area so that janitorial subcontractors cannot undercut one another by paying workers less. In 2016, 2,000 Toronto-area janitors reached a three-year deal with seven of the largest cleaning companies for a 13 percent raise and improvements in benefits and job security.[24]

In the United States, the SEIU has poured tens of millions of dollars into organizing fast-food workers, despite having faint hope of achieving collective agreements in the short term. The "Fight for $15" campaign has organized walkouts and protests by fast-food workers and lobbied various levels of government to mandate a minimum wage of fifteen dollars an hour. California, New York, Seattle, San Francisco, and Washington, DC, have all agreed. By investing millions in this organizing push, SEIU has laid a foundation by building leadership and solidarity across workplaces. Someday, with a more sympathetic federal government and different rules, this could result in unionizing franchises. Canadian unions also participate in "Fight for $15" campaigns, but to date they have not committed resources comparable to those of the SEIU in the United States to invest in organizing fast-food workers themselves, although there has been success lobbying governments to increase the minimum wage.

There are good reasons for unions to organize workers who might never have a collective agreement, whether to help improve their working conditions or to build societal solidarity and political power. Several unions have provisions in their constitutions to grant membership to workers without collective agreements. Unifor's community chapters are one prominent

Canadian example. A group of workers bound by theme or geography can come together and become Unifor members through a community chapter and receive union support and certain benefits. Current examples include a group of United Church ministers and a group of Canadian workers doing freelance communications, neither of whom can achieve a collective agreement but who can nevertheless form a common cause. In Canada, these efforts are relatively modest, with memberships in the hundreds. In contrast, in the United States, the AFL-CIO helped to establish Working America,[25] an affiliate for people who share its broad values and goals, which now has more than 3 million members. Working America works on local issues that its members care about, and it serves as part of a political program to organize in key districts to help elect pro-labour candidates. Further advantages to having direct relationships with so many people are the intelligence and leads generated for organizing new workplaces.

Canada has several worker centres that help non-unionized workers with workplace problems and advocate for economy-wide improvements, such as stronger employment standards laws and higher minimum wage laws. Good examples are the Workers Action Centre in Toronto and the Immigrant Workers Centre of Montreal. The centres help workers to exercise their rights under the laws that do exist, provide education and training sessions, and join with allied organizations to push for legislative change, such as better rights for migrant workers. Worker centres are independent from unions but rely on them for funding. They often take an organizing approach. For example, the Workers Action Centre invites people whom it helps to become members and then invites them to organizing meetings to participate in campaign development. Most of its leaders are drawn from people who went through this process.

To date, the Canadian labour community has not demonstrated the necessary ambition in terms of scale of and creativity in organizing needed to reverse its decline. With two-thirds of the Canadian workforce not belonging to unions, including 85 percent of workers in the private sector, a large amount of concerted organizing is needed. The starting point seems to be fostering a stronger culture of organizing with existing union members so that they can help with the task of organizing new segments of the workforce. Although much greater resources for paid organizers are needed, the labour community won't succeed if it relies solely on paid staff to try to build a movement. The more than 4.5 million existing union members are a great place to begin.

Case Studies

The case studies presented here tackle two aspects of engagement organizing within unions: organizing culture and practice in the case of UNITE HERE Local 75 and digital and data innovation in the case of the BCGEU.

UNITE HERE Local 75: "We Can Win All the Time"

According to President of UNITE HERE Local 75 Lis Pimentel, "the motto of our union is 'Are you having fun, and are you building the committee?'"[26] "If you are not having fun, then you won't be very motivating to people, but, if you are having too much fun, you are not building the committee, and you won't win." Local 75 organizes hospitality workers in the Greater Toronto Area. In researching this book, I asked several members of the labour community which unions are having success lately, and UNITE HERE Local 75 came up repeatedly, not just as a union that is growing, but also as a union that is successfully organizing in ethnically diverse workplaces not at the high end of the income scale.[27] In an industry that often offers only minimum wage, Local 75 has managed to get Toronto-area hotels, 65 percent of which it has unionized, to a standard of about twenty dollars an hour plus full benefits, including pension and dental benefits. How? The union puts bottom-up organizing at the heart of everything that it does. "We are the union that meets," says Organizing Director David Sanders.[28] "We meet a lot!"

UNITE HERE has an unintentionally great name. It resulted from a brief and acrimonious merger of the Hotel Employees and Restaurant Employees International Union (HERE) and the Union of Needletrades, Industrial, and Textile Employees (UNITE). The unions went through a messy divorce, with the UNITE faction leaving, but the name remained. Its organizing culture and method can be traced to New Haven, Connecticut, and to the HERE battle to organize workers at Yale University. HERE has a long history dating back to 1891, when it was known as a bartenders' union. Prohibition in the United States played a role in exposing the union to organized crime, and it wrestled with corruption for a long time until US regulators helped to clean it up.

Vincent Sirabella was a HERE member who quickly gained a reputation for agitating within the union against complacent and ineffective officials. In 1958, he was sent to be the business agent of the almost defunct New Haven local to get him out of the way.[29] There he was free to do things differently. Sirabella already believed in organizing and member involvement and wanted to tap into the energy of other social movements active at the time. He later hired John Wilhelm, who had been a student leader active in anti-war and civil rights causes. Their partnership would end up transforming HERE.

Central to this transformation was use of the committee, HERE's version of the snowflake model of organizing. When HERE was organizing Yale University's clerical workers, one challenge was that there were 2,700 people in small work units spread across 200 buildings. Out of necessity, it developed a much larger organizing committee with people from each work site, no matter how small, and asked a subset of these workers to take responsibility for the organizing drive itself. In breaking new ground and learning from that experience, Wilhelm said, "I think we have a much better understanding of what the function of the organizer actually is, which is not to organize the workers at all but to train the rank-and-file leaders."[30]

Sirabella eventually became director of organizing for the whole union, and the mantra of HERE became "the organizer organizes the committee and the committee organizes the workers."[31] Organizing hotels proved to be more difficult, so HERE added to committee organizing the "comprehensive campaign," in which it researches all the things that a hotel owner needs (e.g., city permits) and leverages this information to get a neutrality agreement in which the employer doesn't oppose unionization. This is like doing a power analysis, which was discussed in Chapter 1. And, given that hotels are part of large international chains, HERE structures contracts and campaigns to engage companies simultaneously wherever they operate.

New Haven was the training ground for many UNITE HERE organizers and leaders, including several who ended up at Local 75 in Toronto, such as Pimentel and Sanders. They have applied the committee organizing structure to add thousands of workers to their membership over the past years, reaching about 8,500 members today and earning a reputation for success. UNITE HERE uses the approach of organizing "organic leaders." As Pimentel explains, people are already organized in their own ways, and the technique is to bring that organization into the union. So you ask some questions. Who is the person who organizes parties? Who runs the lottery pool? Who rides to work with five others every day? Who has been around the longest? Then you find out what these people care about and how the union can be a vehicle for their concerns and recruit them to be committee leaders.

Sanders underlines this message. "You can't control who is a leader in a department. That happens independently," he says. His own history supports this view. In his younger days at Yale University, Sanders was a "terrible union member" with issues around authority. Sometimes he'd let the union organizer advance with initiatives but then put the brakes on things for no good reason, and he could do so because he was an organic leader in his workplace and could bring others along – or not. Local 75 tries to have one committee member for every ten members but more like one for every six during strikes, when more intensive communication is required. There are more formal stewards in the union who are also members of the committee. Through this committee structure, a paid organizer ends up supporting about 1,000 members in an already unionized workplace but is responsible for more like 200 new members during a drive to unionize a workplace. The committees are also federated and send representatives to a citywide executive board that makes decisions for Local 75.

For Pimentel, grievances are "totally the boss's game. There's no way of winning the fight if that's all you are going to do. You need to be able to mobilize people. It's important to do both." Local 75 does file grievances, but it constantly looks for opportunities for members to take action collectively. "We try to enforce collective agreements on the ground," says Sanders. "If you only fight through grievances you will get overwhelmed by the employer since they can outspend you, and it doesn't actually empower workers, because you don't have the experience of beating your boss." So, if a member is fired unfairly, then a grievance can be filed that will take a year to process, or eighty union members can march into the manager's office and demand that things be fixed right away. For Sanders, this comes down to the philosophy of the union: "Your job isn't to represent the workers; your job is to organize the workers to represent themselves." The stronger the union in the workplace, he believes, the less the grievance system is used.

Local 75 tries to engage its members year round, even between unionization battles or contract negotiations. "Sometimes we have a shop where we need a little excitement," says Pimentel. An example was the union mobilizing around the 2014 Ontario election, when opposition leader Tim Hudak promised to weaken labour laws. Local 75 had one of the most active pushback campaigns and signed up 6,000 members and their families to vote no to Hudak. In another example outside the workplace, UNITE HERE worked with community groups in the lower-income Rexdale neighbourhood of Toronto to get a community benefits agreement from a company that wanted to expand a race track where its members worked. Says Sanders: "Members don't just work. Ultimately, the union should be a vehicle for people to exercise control over their lives and where they live."

UNITE HERE starts training people on the job. It takes experienced organic leaders and matches them up with emerging organic leaders in mentoring relationships. It also has more formal training for its leaders and paid organizers. The organizers meet to share lessons and to workshop issues. An example is how to work with more advanced leaders who push back more. In terms of organizers, "if we have a strike, we probably get a staff person out of that," says Pimentel. "The person who helps get folks through a tough fight, who has the chops and motivation to keep learning but is kind of fearless and willing to take on difficult things even though they don't know how to do them – those are the kind of people we tend to hire." Leaders and organizers will be encouraged to move around to other departments or workplaces to stretch themselves. "It's all based on our goals," says Pimentel. "You can't train people for training's sake. Where it works best is where something is going on, where there's clearly something at stake."

Like most unions, UNITE HERE is playing catch up when it comes to data and technology. Although it does have up-to-date contact information for all its members – something that not all unions can claim – its digital systems don't do everything that it wants. The Toronto organizing offices have special paint on their walls to turn them into giant whiteboards to do things such as low-tech member mapping. Sanders says that the local IT person once customized FileMaker Pro to track groups digitally, but the UNITE HERE head office wants everyone on the same system. Although the current database is slow and not designed for what's needed, the broader UNITE HERE union is working on updating systems. Sanders sees the importance of members getting together digitally, particularly during conflicts in which workers need to see representations of themselves not filtered by the media as forms of social proof and in which sharing information quickly can keep the employer in check. He points out that Local 75's recent unionization of Toronto's Rogers Centre and its 1,000 young workers will inject a huge amount of new blood into the digital conversation.

Local 75 builds member committees in the workplace but also works globally. Says Pimentel: "The fight used to be one group of people and one employer. Very bricks and mortar. Now it's much more globalized. In bargaining with Hilton or Hyatt, we have to think about what's going to move them." Enter the power analysis. The union has a research department that helps to develop what's called a "comprehensive campaign" that looks at the entire picture of a company. For example, in exchange for a development permit for a new hotel, Toronto City Council made an agreement with Trump Hotels that it would only require a card check for unionization. The company reneged, though, and UNITE HERE organized anyway, winning the union vote. Local 75 continues to look for these kinds of opportunities, reaching out internationally to help organize hotels in foreign countries and lining up contract expirations to bring maximum pressure to bear. This is necessary since only so many gains are possible in a single workplace before it's out of sync with its competitors. So sustainable gains need to be made industry-wide.

Pimentel and Sanders use the word *win* a lot. The union cultivates a culture of no compromise, of not showing any weakness. "We teach new organizers, if you know you will never give up, you don't need to fear losing," says Sanders. "The only thing you need to worry about is when you are going to win." They are also wary of what happens when members aren't constantly engaged, since this leaves an opening for attacks, not just in one workplace, but also economy-wide. Sanders points to the United States to see what happens when unionization in the private sector drops too far. Non-union members become resentful, and governments then feel free to go after public sector unions.

There are some critiques of UNITE HERE, not necessarily related to Local 75. Some former UNITE HERE organizers in the United States went public with allegations of what's called "pink sheeting": gathering personal information on members (on pink paper) to use to pressure them. This relates to the storytelling practice of people who share their life experiences to make connections to their motivations for acting. An unethical listener could exploit this information later. UNITE HERE variously dismissed the allegations as mischief by its opposition during its bitter divorce or pledged to stamp out the practice if it was happening. Another critique relates to burning out its organizers with its full-on style. As Pimentel admits, "doing what we do is hard. The day to day of it is very intense. We work very hard, long hours and never stop building and fighting and have real struggles with each other and with ourselves. It's very intense sometimes." Sanders tries to counsel that it's a marathon, not a sprint. He likes to use a passage from Nelson Mandela's writing in which Mandela climbs a mountain and then realizes that there are more mountains and valleys as far as the eye can see. You enjoy the view for a while and then get moving again.

The committee system of Local 75 and of UNITE HERE relies heavily on members volunteering. Notable is that the union asks lower-income people of many ethnicities – demographic groups already facing hardship – to volunteer. Sanders believes, though, "if the labour movement is going to be based on paying people to organize, we are never going to win." He sees that people volunteer for all kinds of things all the time, so why not for building your own power? This is reminiscent of the thinking of ACORN. Pimentel articulates a vision beyond the workplace and points to Connecticut, where the organizing style of the union was born and where UNITE HERE now has a strong influence on many political institutions. Says Pimentel: "We aspire to the idea that we can have real power, not just power to transform the workplace but society and politics. We can win all the time."

The BCGEU's "Magical Unicorn of the Sea"

Paul Finch was running in the election for executive office in the BCGEU, the union that represents BC government employees and workers in related sectors such as health care, social services, and education.[32] He had become a member years earlier as a mail clerk in the Ministry of Health. Like all good candidates, he canvassed the voting delegates on what was important to them. Surprisingly, what he heard wasn't about issues of bargaining, wages, or politics. It was that the union didn't have accurate membership lists. Organizers were even hesitant to get new members to sign union cards since they were afraid that those names wouldn't be reflected in the lists that they would later receive. It was a huge problem.

Nearly all unions have data legacy challenges and run on systems designed for different times. Finch traces the legacy issues back even further to the birth of the postwar legal framework, when unions won automatic dues collection and remittance by employers. This was a trade-off. Unions gained financial stability, but now there was little reason for a union steward to talk to all members. A steward's job became to handle grievances for individuals, and connection with the overall membership was lost. Finch saw an opportunity not just to fix the BCGEU's broken membership lists but also to re-establish this connection. "The goal is to change in some ways back to what it was before, but better," he said. In 2014, Finch won election as the BCGEU treasurer in part based upon the promise to fix the union's systems. He hired Jacob Hunter, a marijuana activist who had worked with the municipal party Vision Vancouver on its database system. Together they developed a plan to transform the union's systems and in the process, they hoped, to begin to shift its culture.

Finch and Hunter saw two bad pathways, in some ways mirrors of one another. The first is common to many organizations: different departments use different systems for their functions, whether financial processing, volunteer management, events, or communications. With no integration, these systems can't talk to one another, and the organization ends up with pools of data stranded in different places and spends much time manually transferring information back and forth, also grappling with different formats. The second is systems that want to reconcile this problem by trying to do everything in one place. Hunter says that this leads to the problem that a system is a mile wide but an inch deep, not doing anything particularly well and equivalent to trying to build a house with a Swiss Army knife. Such systems are often unstable and expensive. Says Hunter: "We don't need to live in a world of monolithic databases and duct tape functionality."

Instead, they stole a design idea and a name from the 2012 Barack Obama presidential campaign. The design idea is to have a consistent back-end database in which all information automatically ends up and several front-end applications to perform needed functions. The applications don't need to talk to one another, but they all need to talk to the database. When better applications are found, they replace old ones. Finch and Hunter used the name that the Obama campaign used for the database – Narwhal – what they call "the magical unicorn of the sea." For events and organizing, the BCGEU uses NationBuilder. For dues processing, it uses UnionWare. And for the new conversations that stewards are to have with members, it uses NGP VAN. The data from each system feed back into Narwhal.

With the system upgrade, BCGEU's 2,000 stewards are now asked to have a conversation with every member in their units once or twice a year. Doing so re-establishes the connection lost with dues check off and uses the rationale of updating member information periodically in person. When stewards have these conversations, they have a mobile version of NGP VAN on their smartphones in which they enter answers to questions that they ask members, including contact information updates, surveys on union issues or political questions, and whether the member wishes to be more involved in the union. The steward then hits a button to synchronize the information, reflected in the database within minutes. During the pilot stage, as the system rolled out in two locals, 30 percent of members said yes to becoming more involved in the union, and the local executive then used NGP VAN to follow up with those members in a phone bank to further scope out what that involvement might look like. In this way, the culture of engagement in the union began to shift.

Steward uptake for the new system was good in the pilots, even among older stewards. It takes minimal technical proficiency to use the system. Members are excited by the smartphone app and often want to play with it. The union has doubled its training budget, and all new stewards receive a training module on the system in their orientation. The BCGEU has also directed resources to rural areas to ensure that there is good support for stewards there using the system and to remote workplaces where there might not be stewards.

To better engage its members, the BCGEU also doubled its events budget to provide more opportunities for them. Finch and Hunter developed an engagement ladder to be able to segment communications. The ladder's stages are unaware, aware, attendee, activist, elected. The difference between unaware and aware is whether members open their emails. Although 60 percent are in the unaware category, Finch sees this as par for the course in most unions, since members have been negatively conditioned by being spammed with "horrific" emails with "five pages of text and ten-point font." He and Hunter have set a goal to chip away at this unaware category before the next major round of bargaining, or members will be getting their information from the employer and the media, both of which are usually hostile to the union's cause.

With multiple systems collecting information and feeding it into the same place, thought must be given to protocols for which system gets to overwrite the data of another system. Some systems are designed to receive data from the employer, but what if the data conflict with the information collected by stewards? The BCGEU decided that it would prioritize the stewards' data, even if they ended up being wrong. It is an issue of trust and respect. The union would rather engage in a conversation with a steward to sort things through than see months of his or her work automatically overwritten.

Members access the union website through their own portals. They enter their worksite and geographic location, and they are taken to a page tailored for them where they can update contact information and see information relevant to them personally, such as their collective agreement and any recent news. Hunter helped to build the BCGEU's first version of Narwhal in about two weeks and the second in about four weeks. The union intends to make it available to other unions in the spirit of being an open source. As Finch sees it, "the reason we exist as a union is to serve working people of all kinds."

An example of the new systems in action is a recent battle for a highway maintenance contract in the East Kootenay area of British Columbia. Usually, there are union successor rights for highway contracts, but the government in this case tried to put the bid out to non-unionized companies. In designing a response, the BCGEU needed to know its members' tolerance for various degrees of action, so it conducted a survey via NGP VAN and got results in two days, something that would have taken much longer before. It also put up a petition via NationBuilder and responded with billboards. A seven-year contract ended up being awarded to a company unionized by the BCGEU.

Implementing systems change at the BCGEU wasn't easy, just as change anywhere isn't easy. But Finch likens the evolution to the Iron Age, which destroyed what had been built during the Bronze Age, "which is exactly what will happen with new organizing technology."

Lessons for Engagement Organizing

The period following the Second World War saw great advancements for unions as membership increased and conditions improved. At the same time, a union model that de-emphasized organizing workers in favour of servicing them was locked in. Then, as economic and political circumstances shifted, unions were ill prepared to adapt and membership dropped precipitously. Remaining union members were also less engaged. Observers began to talk about unions "in crisis."

Unions can recapture a more robust version of organizing that they helped to invent decades ago and engage workers of all kinds to build their power, including existing union members, potential union members, and workers who may never get a collective agreement. There are bright spots of success, as seen in the case studies of UNITE HERE and the BCGEU. Unions should aim to:

- *Reclaim a broader definition of organizing.* Unions helped to invent modern organizing, but a servicing model and the grievance process took over. Labour organizing can be reclaimed as building power with workers everywhere – it's never over, even in a workplace with a contract.

- *Catch up with political parties and NGOs in the use of digital tools and data to build power.* Invest in robust systems to establish, manage, and enhance conversations with members to better mobilize and organize.

- *Go bigger and broader in organizing in the new economy.* Bigger investments and more creativity in organizing models are needed to reach the 85 percent of workers in Canada's private sector who don't belong to a union. This will determine whether labour thrives or withers.

chapter 6

Electoral Organizing

> Q: Excuse me. Are you the Judean People's Front?
>
> A: Fuck off! We're the People's Front of Judea!
>
> – Monty Python, *Life of Brian*

"What is the point of a political party?" asks Liberal Party speech writer Colin Horgan.[1] And who are parties for anyway? It's odd that he and others in his party were asking these seemingly philosophical questions right after their victory in the Canadian federal election of 2015. Most newly governing parties would treat their next convention as a celebration and then turn the page to the policy agenda. Instead, the main debate at the convention of the Liberal Party right after its victory was a proposal to get rid of paid party memberships and to streamline the party constitution to become more like a movement.

Critics variously described the proposal as a centralizing power grab, shallow digital populism, or a strategic blunder that would leave the party vulnerable to hostile takeover. Although these criticisms might have had merit, they also reflect a failure to recognize how the breakdown of the broadcast era is fundamentally affecting the nature of political parties, just as it does all institutions, perhaps more so in the case of politics. In functioning democracies, parties seek the approval of as many citizens as possible and get regular and clear feedback every time people vote. This discipline means that parties are hard-wired to respond to underlying shifts in how citizens engage in society and, as we saw in the case of US presidential campaigns, are often laboratories for campaign innovation.

The Liberal Party overthrew the Conservative Party in the 2015 election in large part because of the unpopularity of the incumbent prime minister. But, as we will see in the case study below, it also grasped better than the other main challenging party the underlying shifts in the campaign landscape. Its post-election change to the party constitution was an attempt to lock in that advantage. Whether that succeeds only time will tell, and critics might yet have reason to say "I told you so" should the Liberal Party's claim to want to emulate a movement prove shallow. Indeed, what a movement consists of was never defined. Nevertheless, the trends are there for all parties to capture or be left behind.

Whose Party Is This Anyway?

Parties have always responded to the times because they live or die by keeping up with the public. In the pre-broadcast era, before mass communications existed and when literacy was not universal, parties often relied on a "clientistic" model of providing direct patronage or benefits to persuade voters.[2] This could come in the form of government spending on local projects when in power, government appointments, or even bribes at election time. My father-in-law tells stories of car trunks full of liquor to distribute while working on one party's GOTV operations in the Maritimes. The clientistic model made local and regional party bosses powerful actors in the party as distributors of benefits, gatekeepers to volunteers, and sources of information. Central party leaders needed to keep them onside to be able to win.

The broadcast era allowed parties to get into voters' living rooms to make their cases directly. This approach enhanced the role of the leader as chief spokesperson and took power away from local party officials. Instead, parties began to rely on pollsters to tell them where voters stood. Fundraising became important to buy television time, and political advertising became heavily influenced by marketing practices, likening a party and its leader to a product to be sold and bought like soap.[3] Campaigns begin to distinguish between the work of "persuasion" of voters through mass media by party central and encouraging "turnout" of voters by identifying supporters and getting them to the polls, a task undertaken by local party associations. Local candidates were simply along for the ride.

The breakdown of the broadcast era and the rise of digital tools have begun to shift things again. People's relationships with information and institutions have become more participatory, and their demand for authenticity has gone up, rendering traditional marketing tactics less useful. Researchers such as Donald Green and Alan Gerber have shown that the more personal the communication the more persuasive it is,[4] and Howard Dean showed that it is possible to use the Internet to recruit and mobilize volunteers at scale to talk to people in person. Barack Obama perfected that practice and added advanced data practices to profile and reach people individually. This means that there is now the possibility to move beyond mass communications to individualized communications at a massive scale. The distinction between persuasion and turnout has blurred, with local campaigns positioned to have meaningful conversations with voters and head office equipped with tools to drive people to the polls.

But to whom does a party belong? In one sense, all parties belong to voters on election day, but what about between elections? If a party aspires to be a movement, then it will belong in a meaningful way to some large cross-section of the public, but can that ever be true? Nearly all parties are run day to day by a handful of party insiders, so this becomes a question of their accountability. In the pre-broadcast clientistic model, there was little accountability beyond the ballot box, but it did exhibit tribal-like loyalties – people's political affiliations were wrapped up with their personal or familial identities and fed by patronage. During the broadcast era, there was the veneer of party democracy through paid party memberships. Being a member let you vote to determine your local candidate and your party leader, and in theory play a role in policy formulation, though in practice that was largely ignored. Even then, to regular voters, internal debates by party members sounded a bit like the Monty Python quotation at the start of the chapter – arcane. Once elected party leader, that person and those around her or him pretty much called the shots, including the ability to veto local candidates and dictate party platform.

Today people are less likely either to align their personal identities with a party or to become a member of any kind. Support is now more a function of earning people's participation anew each time. For party brass, this means that their legitimacy will increasingly be driven by their ability to invite real and constant participation and to demonstrate that they are not just listening but also hearing. If party supporters don't sense this responsiveness, then they will cease to be supporters. The Liberals under Justin Trudeau led the way in Canada with this change. In 2013, they created a "supporter" class that did not have to pay for membership but could vote for party leader. Hundreds of thousands signed up as supporters to participate in a leadership vote. At its 2016 convention, the party voted to do away with paid memberships entirely. At the same time, it modernized how it debates policy. President of the Liberal Party Anna Gainey described the old process as "inflexible, it is not evergreen, it does not respond to the pace of life in the digital age."[5]

A note of caution from history is that the Liberal Party flirted with opening itself up before, under Justin's father. During his 1968 election campaign, Pierre Trudeau promised to practise "participatory democracy." He commissioned a process to ask the party's grassroots for policy ideas, but then summarily ignored them, significantly damaging party morale.[6] Whether his son repeats the cycle remains to be seen. Early in his government, there were signs of opening decision making across cabinet and the civil service,[7] but much of this was relative to the prior prime minister, who had centralized everything in his office. A worrying sign was that, in the first year of the new mandate, a record number of lobbyists registered in Ottawa,[8] which can reinforce the perception that special interests that can afford lobbyists are setting the agenda rather than ordinary citizens in a real movement. Early on, the Trudeau government also struggled to wean itself off "cash for access" political fundraisers, which made ministers available to socialize with high donors, breaking a high-profile promise to make Canada's electoral system more fair, both of which eroded confidence that the Liberal Party was truly committed to being different.

Laws governing elections shape organizing incentives and disincentives for parties. On the one hand, Canada's antiquated first-past-the-post voting system forces national parties to form coalitions of voters in the 40 percent range in order to form the government. On the other, it forces parties to focus on areas that they can win, thereby reducing efforts to organize with voters elsewhere. The Canadian election finance system builds a wall between local constituency campaigns and the leader's campaign, with separate spending caps for each. This is a vestige of the separation of persuasion and turnout functions, which no longer holds today.

Although parties might be limited in some ways by election laws, this is not true for data.[9] Unlike in the United States, where lists of voters are public, in Canada political parties have exclusive access to such data and face fewer privacy restrictions than companies or NGOs. The Conservative Party pioneered the practice of gathering information on every Canadian (not just members or supporters), giving each a score for estimated level of support, but other parties are now caught up in this practice. The pervasiveness of data use by parties raises ethical flags, particularly without the knowledge and permission of voters. At the same time, it opens the door to parties not only talking to voters as individuals but also listening to them.

Earlier we saw how the Howard Dean campaign of 2004 "plowed snow" for others that followed, including the campaigns of Obama and Sanders. Each of these campaigns used engagement organizing practices to varying degrees to help mobilize hundreds of thousands of volunteers to engage in one-on-one voter contact. The Obama campaigns developed a culture of testing and data gathering to measure the impact of everything they did so that it could be improved. In 2016, the Bernie Sanders campaign continued to innovate and developed a faster and more digitally distributed buildout of volunteer campaign infrastructure that it dubbed "Big Organizing." Even Donald Trump bucked his own party's establishment with an appeal to (often ugly) populism, fueled by social media and by large rallies. What about elsewhere? In Europe, there are also examples of political parties reinventing themselves for the post-broadcast era that are more movement-like than either the US examples or the Canadian Liberal Party. This might be because of a different electoral system that lets parties be more true to an enthusiastic constituency and not get penalized for it at the ballot box. Two of the most notable are the Five Star Movement in Italy and Podemos in Spain.

The Five Star Movement, or Movimento Cinque Stelle (M5S), is a political party born out of frustration with traditional Italian parties' inability to deal with issues such as corruption, the financial crisis, and the environment. Its founder, comedian Beppe Grillo, frequently criticized politicians in his comedy acts before meeting web strategist Gianroberto Casaleggio, who encouraged him in 2004 to start a blog. When it took off, and inspired by the Dean campaign, they began to use Meetup to foster local events, with hundreds of groups forming. In 2007, Grillo held the first Vaffanculo (meaning "fuck off") Day, or V-Day, to collect signatures to petition the parliament for anti-corruption legislation. The V would be incorporated into the logo of the M5S party, with the five stars standing for the issues of public water, sustainable transportation, sustainable development, Internet access, and environmentalism.

The party promotes direct democracy, with supporters helping to develop policies online and selecting party candidates through online primaries. Candidates can serve only two terms and cannot have criminal records. The party often shuns mainstream media, partly because of its philosophy of using the Internet and partly because of the Italian legacy of media control by Silvio Berlusconi, the disgraced former prime minister. After 2008, M5S began to have success at the municipal level and elected several mayors in major cities. The party came second in the 2013 national election, with almost 9 million votes, and refused to partner with other parties to govern the country. Grillo's role in the party appears to be mixed: Grillo doesn't run for office himself, so the party is leaderless, but in practice he makes many decisions and has been accused of being undemocratic.

The new Spanish political party Podemos (meaning "we can") was born from the social movement that inspired Occupy Wall Street. On May 15, 2011, demonstrations took place in fifty-eight Spanish cities in response to the economic crisis, the role of the banks, and the government's austerity agenda. It was called the 15-M movement or the Indignados (meaning "indignant"). Tens of thousands of people took part in occupying squares, hosting assemblies, and challenging the consensus of the mainstream parties – "they don't represent us."[10] Although the protests didn't last, they did find an outlet in *la Tuerka,* an online political TV show produced by a Madrid professor named Pablo Iglesias. He believed that many of Spain's problems resulted from the political and economic "caste" that ran the country, including politicians and bankers in the European Union. His notoriety grew as a television personality, and Iglesias turned his attention to entering politics: "The logic of the 15-M movement led to its exhaustion; it didn't achieve the effects desired by its committed activists, who hoped that the social could substitute for the institutional."[11]

Iglesias approached existing political parties on the left to encourage them to run open primaries, "to look more like the people," but he was rebuffed.[12] So he decided in 2014 to launch Podemos, a party that would carry forward themes of the 15-M movement. It would also retain 15-M-style assemblies around the country, including meeting online. Podemos supporters used the Internet to rank party candidates for the 2014 European Union election, and the party took 8 percent of the vote, electing five people, including Iglesias. The party continued to develop digital tools, including voting tools and an online debating forum called Plaza Podemos, which attracts between 10,000 and 20,000 people daily.[13] In the 2015 national election, Podemos received about a fifth of the vote, coming third after just two short years in existence and challenging Spain's two-party system. In 2015, Podemos staged a March for Change with hundreds of thousands of people in the streets of Madrid, with the goal to "end the disassociation between mass and electoral politics."[14]

In reviewing examples of new, more digitally driven parties around the world, it is interesting that each features a charismatic leader with a high level of authenticity. Dean, Obama, Sanders, Grillo, and Iglesias all fit this mould, as do Naheed Nenshi and Justin Trudeau in the case studies that follow. This fits with the public's new relationships with information and institutions and its heightened desire for authenticity. It also raises interesting questions about the fluid boundaries between bottom-up participation and top-down leadership. Elements of both appear to be important to political success. A party's theory of change is determined in part by the logic of elections themselves – if you get more votes than the others, then you form the government. But another part of it concerns the leader – if she or he leads the government, then we trust her or him to include us in what happens next.

This is a critical point in the debate about political populism. Britain's vote to leave the EU and Trump's election are held up as examples of bad things that have happened due to growing populism, but such critiques flirt with being undemocratic. While increased populism is likely here to stay, the real question is how politicians will react to it. There will be those who stoke fear (often along tribal lines) and present themselves as an antidote, while building a mobilizing movement based on dependency on the leader.

The alternative is a movement based on true organizing, which builds agency and autonomy of voters themselves to take on challenges together. This can also be seen as a form of populism, but with "all the difference in the world."[15]

There is the question of maintaining movement-like participation should a party form the government. Neither Dean nor Sanders needed to answer that question, and at the time of writing the Five Star Movement and Podemos have yet to attain high office. The Obama campaigns are more instructive. In 2008, Obama's large and initially enthusiastic volunteer network was encouraged to continue its work as part of Organizing for America, an initiative run by the Democratic Party. There volunteers were asked to work to build support for government policy initiatives such as health-care reform. But there was a tension with the logic of volunteering essentially as an arm of the government, and interest waned. After the 2012 campaign, a different approach was chosen. Volunteers became part of Organizing for Action, which had no formal affiliation with either the Democratic Party or Obama. Organizing for Action allowed people not only to work for government initiatives if they chose but also to branch out to other campaigns to maintain their enthusiasm. Overall, it kept organizers in the field organizing.

Case Studies

Below are two Canadian case studies of electoral campaigns that teach engagement organizing lessons. The 2010 Naheed Nenshi campaign for mayor of Calgary was the first significant political campaign in Canada that used the Internet to foster both online and offline participation, including a grassroots-organizing effort. The 2015 federal election campaign was the first time that at least two major Canadian political parties tried to adapt the lessons of the Obama presidential campaigns, with varying degrees of success.

Nenshi's Purple Dawn

In the wee hours of election day, hundreds of volunteers for the Naheed Nenshi 2010 campaign for mayor of Calgary hit the streets of the city with purple chalk to write the campaign's "Better Ideas" on sidewalks. It was the culmination of a remarkable campaign in which their candidate went from having no money, no recognition, and no chance in a field of fifteen candidates to beating out two well-resourced and well-known establishment contenders. The volunteers dubbed the early morning push "Operation Purple Dawn" after the campaign colour that by then was everywhere. The idea itself came from a volunteer, which reflected the open and innovative nature of the campaign. That evening Nenshi would become Canada's first Muslim mayor in a city with a historical reputation for being true blue conservative. Not purple.

Before launching into the story of Nenshi's first campaign for mayor, there is a caveat. Nenshi won because "he was the right candidate at the right time," says campaign manager Chima Nkemdirim. "Calgary was looking for a leader like Naheed – they just didn't know it yet," he said.[16] Luck also broke Nenshi's way, with vote splits and weak campaign choices hurting his ideological competitors.[17]

Election managers are usually taught a campaign logic based upon a finite universe of voters. Start with the voters list, identify "your" and "their" core supporters to turn out the former, and identify voters to persuade. Set measurable targets to recruit the right number of volunteers to talk to the right number of voters in the right places. But Nenshi friend and adviser Brian Singh likens the 2010 campaign logic instead to epidemiology, using virality and transmission mechanisms to spread a (good) disease by exponential growth.[18]

Although Nenshi was relatively unknown to the public, he was well known to what the campaign called "hyper-engaged" civic politics watchers. In 2004, he had run to be a city councillor and lost. As a professor at Mount Royal University, he was active in groups with a focus on civic renewal, and he was a frequent media commentator on city issues and politics. The campaign decided to recruit and mobilize the hyper-engaged as a first circle of evangelists to begin the process of infecting the city using word of mouth. It was partly an admission of weakness: the Nenshi campaign didn't have enough money to reach voters via traditional advertising. So it would unleash a grassroots movement that would sweep the city.

Favoured to win the mayor's chair was Ric McIver, a city councillor and traditional conservative with a big campaign war chest. McIver was joined in the race by Barb Higgins, a well-known television personality backed by senior advisers from the centre-right of the political spectrum. Twelve other candidates plus Nenshi made for a crowded field. Six months out from election day the campaign mapped a strategy that wanted Nenshi to be in third place by Thanksgiving, just before the election. That way he'd be the topic of conversation at the dinner table. Singh says that the campaign knew that McIver's one-third of the electorate was solid, but beyond that everything was up for grabs. If the campaign could hold McIver to his base and exceed that number, it would win.

As campaign communications director Richard Einarson describes it, the campaign began "literally with no money. Like zero."[19] Out of necessity, it used social media to get in the game. From his role as a media commentator, Nenshi already had a good online following, and in May he used Twitter and Facebook to announce that he was running for mayor. Reflecting the candidate's policy wonk personality, the campaign decided that it would speak "in full sentences," an expression adapted from the TV program *The West Wing* and, as Nenshi defines it, "actually telling people that we're ready for detailed discussions about complicated issues, and we're not boiling it down to simple solutions and bullet points."[20] This authenticity was critical to recruiting the hyper-engaged, who had detailed opinions that they wanted to offer. For a platform, the campaign developed twelve "Better Ideas," with the word *ideas* implying a conversation, and actively solicited feedback. When the campaign released an idea, it asked the question "Is this a good idea?" and didn't hide negative feedback. In this way, the campaign shared ownership of its policy ideas with the next tier of evangelists.

But Nenshi needed more to stand out with the broader public. Einarson was given the task of developing campaign materials and drafted a blue-and-gold website that he hated. He knew that the two traditionally safe campaign colours in Calgary were blue and green and imagined a sea of similarly coloured campaign signs at busy intersections when all the mayoral, council, and school board candidates had their campaign signs up. Something different was needed. Einarson hit on what he thought was the "really bizarre" idea to use purple as a distinctive colour with few political associations, other than for US swing states that were a blend of Republican red and Democratic blue. He thought that this was fitting for Nenshi, who landed somewhere between the usual conservative and liberal labels. A debate ensued within the campaign team about whether purple would get them laughed out of the election, but the decision was made to try it. Tens of thousands of purple buttons, lawn signs, t-shirts, and bumper magnets were printed up to go along with a new purple website and purple social media branding.

The campaign threw its doors open to volunteers. It was the early days of social media, so there was training on how to use Facebook and how to share online with friends. Volunteers were encouraged not to use talking points but to tell others why they personally supported Nenshi. Digital ads were used to drive likes on the Nenshi campaign Facebook page, and used to promote posts to friends of friends, consistent with the campaign's logic of using virality in the hope of achieving exponential growth. At orientations, volunteers were given purple t-shirts, lawn signs, and bumper magnets and were encouraged to reach out to friends.

The campaign worked hard offline too. Nenshi and volunteers appeared throughout the summer at every event possible, from parades to markets, from church basements to synagogues, with the team's purple t-shirts prominent. Unlike other candidates, Nenshi went to talk to students even if they were too young to vote. The theory was that kids would go home and talk to their parents about the candidate. The campaign began a program of coffee parties in people's houses at which Nenshi would engage with groups ranging in size from five to twenty. Because of his keen mind and engaging personality, the campaign knew that it needed to get Nenshi in front of as many people as possible to let his likability shine. People at coffee parties became strong converts and again were encouraged to reach out to their friends. The coffee parties were part of another of the campaign's core strategies, as described by Nenshi: "Go to citizens where they live and engage them in conversation. Get them talking to one another. And I really, really, believe that's what happened."[21] As the volunteer base grew, the campaign reached out in a variety of ways, including on doorsteps. Rather than being given scripts or talking points, door knockers were encouraged to read through the campaign's Better Ideas and choose which ones they wanted to discuss.[22]

The conversation continued online. Nenshi himself and others in the campaign engaged in a back and forth on Twitter and Facebook. The other campaigns had basic websites, but they barely engaged in social media other than to use it to make announcements. "We used social media like a telephone," Nkemdirim said. "They used it like television. That made the difference."[23] The campaign kept growing its online presence, increasing its Facebook likes through word of mouth and digital ads.

Momentum took time to build. Three months out from the election an opinion poll came out showing Nenshi at about 1 percent support. But, from the perspective of an insurgency campaign, Nkemdirim said, "we were thrilled we were included on the poll."[24] Things started to pick up. Einarson remembers going to a mall and seeing a purple button. He had a hypothesis about grassroots campaign swag: when people see a campaign billboard, at some level they know that it means a candidate "just has rich friends." But when they see a button or a bumper magnet, it counts more as a personal endorsement.

Although the campaign used social media and grassroots outreach to get in the game, Singh notes that "later on we had to be able to nail down a lot of traditional media at the point of decision." Donations started to pick up, and with its philosophy of transparency the campaign published the names of donors. When this didn't happen quickly enough, donors would call to complain. Endorsing Nenshi had become cool. One fundraising email raised the startling amount of about $60,000. The campaign mocked up radio ads and asked people to donate to get them on the air. Einarson believes that the pitch was so successful because donors had told their friends about Nenshi and wanted him on the radio so that they could feel more legitimate in their choice.

Momentum was shifting. Nenshi's major competitors released their platforms late, around Labour Day, hoping to generate media attention closer to the election date. But the Nenshi campaign had been talking about issues for months already, and in much greater detail, so the competitors' ideas seemed to be thin in comparison. About a month before the election, Nenshi started pulling away from the rest of the thirteen less competitive candidates and into a clear third place behind his two major opponents. This legitimized the campaign in the eyes of local media and gave it its wish – to be talked about at the Thanksgiving dinner table. Right before election day, polls showed Nenshi in a dead heat with McIver and Higgins.

Toward the end, the campaign passed 10,000 Facebook likes, a big deal in 2010. It had about 20,000 contactable people. Phone numbers had been collected online and at coffee parties, and the campaign planned a final weekend phone bank. Then tragedy struck as the phone system crashed. The system service provider had sent its people home for the weekend. Nkemdirim went to a mall to get a pack of cellphones to use, and the campaign eventually tracked down the vice-president of the service provider to get him to go fix the system. The campaign released a last video with Nenshi encouraging people to get out and vote. Despite now having money, the campaign kept the feel of the video homegrown, with Nenshi standing in front of hand-written notes on flip charts.

Einarson sent six emails out on the last day encouraging people to vote and tell their friends to do so. He had surreptitiously subscribed to the other campaigns' email lists and was wondering why they weren't sending him anything. "They just didn't get it," he said. The Nenshi campaign had been open book about what it was doing, and its competitors could have stolen its tactics, but they didn't. Einarson realized that, "as long as you are moving, it doesn't matter. It only matters if they are ahead of you." Volunteers fanned out across the city to put up voting reminder notices, including information on where to vote. "Operation Purple Dawn" wiped out all the chalk supplies at Toys R Us and covered city sidewalks with purple.

On the evening of the election, the candidate and campaign volunteers jammed into a bar to wait for the results. It was so loud that Nenshi couldn't hear the television, but he saw Nkemdirim being interviewed and looking happy, and he saw his sister across the room looking emotional. He thought "I'm going to win. And I've got about three minutes to figure out what I'm going to say, because this bar is going to collectively lose its mind."[25] To his credit, as mayor Nenshi has continued to invite Calgarians into the conversation and to participate in running their city. Calgary City Hall receives six times as many calls, emails, and letters as before his election.[26] Nenshi started the "Three Things" campaign to encourage Calgarians to do civic-minded things to help out locally, even something such as shovelling a neighbour's driveway. He regularly responds to people on his Twitter feed, even though he now has over 300,000 followers. In the 2013 municipal election, he was re-elected with 74 percent of the vote.

Nkemdirim cautions that a Nenshi-style campaign won't work for everyone. "Voters are looking for authenticity, so don't try to be the social media candidate if you hate social media," he says. Instead, design a campaign to play to your strengths. One Calgary writer concluded of the 2010 campaign that "it wasn't because we agreed with everything Naheed Nenshi said or believed his vision would be reality overnight; it was because – for some of us, maybe for the first time – we felt fully included in the conversation."[27]

The 2015 Canadian Election: Storming the Castle

The 2015 Canadian election would be a three-way race for once. Usually, the Liberals and Conservatives slug it out for forming the government, and the NDP picks up a few seats. This time the NDP started with the second greatest number of seats and narrowly topped the polls. After ten years of a Conservative government, most Canadians were ready for change. Meanwhile, the Conservatives could count on about a third of the electorate and, with the right vote splits in a first-past-the-post electoral system, could squeak back into power. The real question was whether the "change" vote would consolidate behind a challenger and, if so, which one.

This was the first Canadian election in which both the Liberals and the NDP would more seriously apply lessons learned from US presidential campaigns. Both drew on Obama consultants to advise them on voter contact. Both had updated data systems and applied advanced modelling to the electorate. Both expanded their volunteer field operations and invested in digital campaigning. Ultimately, though, one would execute – and organize – better than the other, with a bit of luck thrown in because of an extra-long official campaign period that allowed it to seal the deal.

The Liberals' preparation began two and a half years earlier with the election of Justin Trudeau as party leader. The Liberals had dropped to third place in Parliament after a decade of intra-party fighting and a series of shaky leaders. Trudeau came with the celebrity status of his father as the former prime minister. The party opened its leadership race by creating a "supporter" category of people who could vote in the contest without taking out a ten dollar membership. Trudeau's famous name helped to bring in tens of thousands of new people who would serve as a strong base to draw on for campaign volunteers. After the 2015 election, the Liberal Party voted to do away with memberships entirely to become more like a movement. "This is something the Liberal party has needed for a long, long time, to remember how to connect with people," said Trudeau.[28]

His team began to remake the party. They brought in a fundraiser from the NGO sector who relied heavily on digital tools and data to increase the number of small donors and to almost double the net haul over a two-year period. Donors were thanked and further engaged "because they are not only donors, they are supporters, ambassadors and voters."[29] The Liberals were determined to run a data-driven campaign. "Some of us had the pleasure of spending time debating every metric. From eyeballs on Facebook versus YouTube videos, to ratios to door knocks to phone calls, from radio ad buys against TV ad buys, and which baseball game more Canadians might be watching," said campaign co-chair Katie Telford. "We spent our days and many nights talking about numbers and turning each one of them into a meaningful element of the campaign."[30]

Canadian veterans of the Obama campaigns who were active Liberals convinced party brass to mimic Obama's volunteer snowflake structure by setting up neighbourhood teams.[31] Almost two years before the election, in early 2014, the party hired fifteen organizers to form the Alpha Team, and each was assigned from five to ten ridings of the 100 Liberal target ridings for the upcoming election. Their job was to use house parties and one-on-one meetings to identify at least one community team leader in each riding to lay the foundation for local voter contact. The Obama veterans started training sessions across the country called Campaign College to revamp how volunteers were brought into the campaign and given responsibilities. Door knockers were coached to give a personal pitch at the door about why they were supporting the Liberals.

The party set formal targets for volunteer recruitment. Teams were to recruit captains for data gathering, canvassing, and phone calling, with some also having "comfort captains" who cooked and cared for the others. In the fall of 2014, the Liberals started using NGP VAN, a voter contact system with a mobile app for canvassers to use on the doorstep to record data. This allowed the campaign to track in real time which candidates were hitting their targets as well as to log voter ID and other information. The data were fed back into the Liberal database. Early in 2015, the party held a day of action with 30,000 voter contact attempts. Then, over one weekend in May, 3,500 volunteers knocked on 200,000 doors in 190 ridings.[32] Around this time, however, the party courted controversy by supporting the heavy-handed security legislation of the Conservative government. Party pollsters argued that this wasn't hurting the party with average voters, but the field team saw a drop in volunteer enthusiasm and recruitment. Furthermore, the NDP formed the government in the spring provincial election in Alberta, which gave voters permission to see the NDP as a viable federal party too. The Liberals dropped in the polls.

A Beta Team of more Liberal national field organizers was hired in the spring of 2015 and another forty or so deputy organizers in the summer. A team of about ten student organizers was also hired to work on campuses. The Liberal campaign leadership actively cultivated a culture of voter contact, frequently tweeting "go knock doors." By the first week in September, the campaign had knocked on over 5 million doors since Trudeau had become the party leader.[33] When the election formally began, spending rules changed, and many of the hired organizers became riding campaign managers instead. There were tensions with some of the more traditional riding managers unfamiliar with the neighbourhood team model. One manager turned a volunteer voter contact team into a team managing sign distribution instead. During the election period, there were varying degrees of success keeping team structures in place.

The NDP also began planning for the election early but had to deal with the untimely death of its leader, Jack Layton, and the selection of a new one. "After Jack died, we lost a couple of years," said James Pratt, who ran the NDP field campaign for the election.[34] The NDP set the goal of retaining its existing seats and targeted another thirty-five ridings where it could pick up new seats.[35] The party was as determined as the Liberals to run a data-driven campaign and had a new database called Populous. The NDP hired Jeremy Bird as an adviser. He had run Obama's 2012 field campaign and underlined the importance of numbers in voter contact – of having targets and of counting everything. There was skepticism within the party about the applicability of the Obama snowflake structure of neighbourhood teams. Pratt thought that the United States was dealing with smaller districts and that American campaigns had more money to hire organizers to support the teams. One NDP candidate in Toronto was herself a trainer in the snowflake model and set up distributed teams in her riding between the time of her nomination and the election call. But, once the campaign was formally under way, her campaign collapsed the teams to run things with a more traditional mobilizing model.[36] Other NDP candidates, particularly in a few ridings in the Vancouver region, did give their volunteers more responsibility, but this appeared to be the exception to the rule.

Like the Liberals, the NDP ran "days of action" to both recruit new volunteers and to get existing volunteers to do more. There is valuable voter contact done at these events, but "the main goal is to get volunteers used to that level of work," said Pratt. Canvassers were identified and trained who stuck with the campaign through election day. Instead of using a mobile app for voter contact, NDP canvassers stuck with clipboards and were encouraged to enter the data right away to complete the job and to feel a sense of accomplishment. The campaign emphasized the theory of change behind voter contact and data entry so that volunteers were motivated. The campaign hired an organizer for every province and sometimes regional organizers for big cities to ensure that local campaigns were on track to meet their targets. When local NDP campaigns hit voter contact targets, the central office would reward them with things such as free access to the central phone bank, for which campaigns would ordinarily have to pay.[37] This provided an incentive for local campaigns to step up.

For voter modelling and targeting, the Liberals combined their own voter contact data with internal polling and other demographic data to give predictive scores from one through ten to everybody on the voters list.[38] The party created an analytics dashboard called The Console to be able to manipulate variables to see, for example, which ridings or which neighbourhoods were put in play with shifts in polling numbers.[39] The party also used the system to develop a health score for each local campaign based upon polls, door knocks, phone calls, and campaign funds.[40] With this knowledge, it could shift resources or people around to help. "It's about ... being able to make smart, strategic decisions that are based on something that is more than just the traditional ways, which was really kind of a combination of high-level polling and kind of gut instinct," said Liberal National Director Jeremy Broadhurst.[41]

The NDP did similar modelling to give a score to each voter, based upon his or her likelihood to support the party. Dan Pollock ran the analytics program for the NDP, and overall he found the modelling a success, with a couple of caveats.[42] First, the party was late in completing it and getting it into the hands of the local campaigns, which in some cases had already started coarser poll targeting rather than individualized targeting. Second, the NDP's modelling ended up working much better in NDP-Conservative races than in three-way races with the Liberals included. The long campaign period didn't help either since there was more time for the landscape to shift under the model.

By the end of the campaign, the NDP counted about 40,000 volunteers compared with the Liberals' 80,000. The NDP had 2.8 million conversations with voters compared with the Liberals' 3.8 million. One Liberal estimated that the party's volunteers provided about $3 million worth of voter contact.[43]

The Conservatives unintentionally gave Trudeau a boost in authenticity. They spent millions of dollars on ads attacking him as "just not ready" and focusing on his personality. Instead of trying to change the focus, the Trudeau campaign responded directly with disarming ads featuring a comfortable-looking Trudeau saying "I'm ready" while looking right into the camera. It helped that he held his own in the leaders' debates, and the campaign constantly put him on streets and at rallies, mingling with crowds and seeming to enjoy it. In contrast, the NDP campaign started badly on the authenticity front. Its leader, Tom Mulcair, was best known as a fiery prosecutor in Parliament and in the past had received good reviews as he held the prime minister to account during Question Period. But, at the first election event, the NDP refused to let him answer media questions and created the impression that he was being managed. During debates, Mulcair seemed to pull punches out of fear of being perceived as an angry person and instead wore a smile that people found forced. While the Liberals let Trudeau be Trudeau, the NDP didn't let Mulcair be Mulcair.

The Liberals were also helped in the battle to win the "change" label when the NDP pledged to stick to balanced budgets, while the Liberals said that they would run deficits. This allowed the Liberals more room to justify their platform promises financially while arguing that the NDP weren't being straight. "We weren't going to tell people that you could have your cake and eat it too," said Liberal campaign co-chair Gerald Butts. "We were being honest."[44] The Liberals also attacked the NDP, alleging that it said one thing in French in Quebec and a different thing in English elsewhere, while also digging into the NDP leader's past, when Mulcair had said supportive things about Margaret Thatcher and bulk water exports, positions antithetical to those of his current party.[45] The Liberals were attacking his authenticity.

The Liberals invested significantly more in digital work than the other parties. Spending records show that, outside traditional advertising, the Liberals spent about $8.8 million on digital advertising and digital voter contact, while the Conservatives spent $5.1 million on paid phone banks.[46] Criticizing this Conservative tactic, Butts said that "the key weakness in that was that it was not real people talking to real people. It was people that they paid."[47] The Liberal digital director estimates that his campaign reached 18 million Canadians online, more than half the population, with content tailored by demographic factors. He notes that a quarter of younger voters use cellphones rather than landlines and that 42 percent no longer watch TV or are light viewers. "If we're going to remain competitive, we clearly need to find new ways of reaching our supporters," he said.[48] Internal party figures indicate that the Liberals' digital ads were viewed 343 million times during the campaign, and the digital team produced more than fifty pieces of content a day.[49] At its height, the Liberal data team numbered fifty people.[50]

The NDP had its main digital success in fundraising. Between July and September 2015, it had 78,227 individual donors, most of whom gave online. This was the largest number of donors in any quarter by any Canadian political party in history.[51] The party raised $7.2 million online in 2015 and $4 million by email. The party even raised more money with a mistake.[52] It asked via email for a five dollar donation, which inadvertently became a fifty dollar donation when the donor clicked on a link to the donation page. But this resulted in higher donations, so the party experimented with sending the mistake to a group of donors and netted 32 percent more revenue compared with that of a control group. The party tested all of its online activities, optimizing its signup page to get 40 percent more RSVPs and experimenting with font size – the larger the better. But the NDP noticed that the Liberals were doing better than it digitally outside fundraising. "Every time there was a debate, social media was full of Liberals," said Pollock. The NDP didn't prioritize organizing via digital channels or engaging people online much beyond fundraising and encouraging them to go to rallies.

Polls show that the Conservatives held largely steady with just under a third of the electorate throughout the election. The movement between the two main opposition parties was the story. That the Conservatives had called a long election campaign was a lucky break for the Liberals, since the "change"

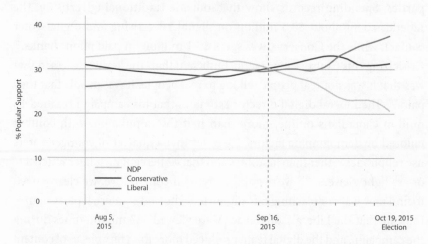

CANADIAN ELECTION POLLING, 2015

Figure 4 This figure shows the shift in popular support for the three main parties in the 2015 federal election. Notable is how the Conservatives started and finished steady with just under a third of the vote, while the real shift took place between the NDP and the Liberals – steady at first and then accelerating close to election day.

Source: Opinion Polling in the Canadian Federal Election, 2015, https://en.wikipedia.org/wiki/Opinion_polling_in_the_Canadian_federal_election,_2015.

voters shifted steadily toward them and away from the NDP, but this took more time than a traditional campaign period. For a while, it seemed that a minority government was likely since no party could consolidate enough of the vote, but then the steady shift turned into a rout. The NDP and many pundits believe that this started in Quebec because of Mulcair's support for letting Muslim women wear a niqab in citizenship ceremonies, an unpopular position in Quebec on an issue that the Conservatives had purposely engineered. Some dispute this interpretation and say that the Liberals did a better job than the NDP in speaking to valid pocketbook issues and convincing voters in Quebec that the Liberals were "real."[53] Nonetheless, as support for the NDP dropped in Quebec, this sent a signal to "change" voters across the country that the Liberals were best able to beat the unpopular Conservatives. The Liberals had already laid the foundation through better voter contact work than the other parties.

Toward the end of the race, Trudeau was drawing big crowds. The campaign staged a huge rally in Brampton, Ontario, and captured TV footage for an ad that used the crowd to make it seem like a movement. "I knew this was over when we showed up in Napanee [in Ontario], to pour coffee at a Tim Hortons and there were 400 people in a parking lot," one adviser travelling with Trudeau said.[54] The Liberals won 184 seats, the Conservatives 99, the NDP 44, the Bloc Québécois 10, and the Green Party 1. Voter turnout jumped by more than 7 percent. Among those aged eighteen to twenty-four, turnout jumped by over 18 percent. There were 1.5 million more voters under thirty-five than in the prior election.[55]

Overall, the Liberals did a better job than the NDP of fostering distributed leadership among volunteers and practising networked communications, but neither party approached the level of sophistication seen in US presidential races. In its postmortem on the election, the NDP faulted itself for misreading the mood of the nation and presenting "cautious change" in contrast to Trudeau's "real change."[56] The NDP still ran its second most successful campaign ever, with its biggest ground game, the most money, and its second highest seat count. Pollock notes that, like the Conservatives of ten years earlier, the Liberals took more risks because they had less to lose – their thirty-four seats going in were totally safe, and in many ways the party was starting fresh. "We have the problem that we don't die enough when we lose," Pollock says. "Losing badly gives you space to reinvent." This is what political scientists call "out party innovation incentives," in which campaign innovation is driven by those who see themselves storming the castle rather than by those who see themselves trying to protect the status quo.[57] Liberal campaign co-chair Butts seems to be aware of this: "Our campaign for 2015 won't work for 2019, we've got to invent it from scratch. We've got to question all the things that we did wrong, but most importantly we've got to question all the things we did right."[58]

Lessons for Engagement Organizing

Political parties are attuned to the underlying shifts in the electorate brought about by the erosion of the broadcast era, and they are adapting to these shifts. Some are trying to become more like a movement, but time will tell whether there are meaningful efforts to share involvement and decision making in parties with their voting constituencies, particularly when in power. Here are some lessons for political parties and electoral actors from engagement organizing:

- *Give more of the party over to its constituency.* Open the party up to meaningful participation and engagement by those from whom the party wants to earn votes and not just party insiders.

- *Shift from mass communication to individualized communication at a massive scale.* The more personal the voter contact, the more effective it is: use data and distributed teams at scale to talk to voters.

- *Be authentic.* Broadcast-era marketing has given way to politicians being themselves, warts and all. Voters want genuine, not packaged, candidates. Campaign accordingly.

Conclusion: Getting Started

You will have to experiment and try things out for yourself
and you will not be sure of what you are doing.
That's all right, you are feeling your way into the thing.

– Emily Carr

Over the past six chapters, I have explored how the erosion of the broadcast era and the rise of digital tools and culture are creating a new campaign landscape. People have a more participatory orientation toward information, and like-minded supporters are easier to find than ever before. Using good organizing practices a campaign can forge solidarity among people, find and cultivate leaders, and build constituencies aligned around a mission. Scaling up quickly is possible by fostering distributed leadership and networked communications. NGOs, unions, and electoral actors can use engagement organizing ingredients to win campaigns.

It is customary to end books like this with inspiration, but common to both the tradition of organizing and the emerging culture of digital campaigning is the practice of assessment, reflection, and honesty about challenges. If we want to win campaigns more often, then we need to understand what we're doing well and what we can do better. We need to understand our strengths and weaknesses and the opportunities and threats that we face.

Without this understanding, we learn less and lose more. And if we lose more, then what is the point of campaigning? To conclude, then, I explore some challenges and trends so that we have our eyes open wide and are ready to overcome barriers. I end with a section on getting started and a recap of lessons drawn from prior chapters.

Challenges and Trends

Challenge: Organizer's Entropy

Community organizing has been around for decades, and digital tools have been available for more than fifteen years, so why isn't the world organized by now? One reason is organizer's entropy. In physics, entropy is a measure of the energy in a system no longer available for doing useful work. Organizers don't like to talk about it, but in their context most human groups that they help to create will naturally tend toward disorder and inactivity. This is organizer's entropy. It happens for several reasons. First, most humans would rather relax and hang out with friends and family members than donate their time and energy to solving problems. As comedian Tina Fey's character in *30 Rock* says, "I believe that all anyone really wants in this life is to sit in peace and eat a sandwich."[1] There are exceptions, of course, particularly if friendships are formed through organizing and if fun is had through acting and winning together. Good organizers will do their best to ensure that they happen.

But organizing isn't all fun and winning. It also involves drudgery, tension, and controversy. As President of UNITE HERE Lis Pimentel said, "Doing what we do is hard. The day to day of it is very intense. We work very hard, long hours and never stop building and fighting and have real struggles with each other and with ourselves. It's very intense sometimes." During the inevitable times when the bad outweighs the good, people will question their participation and let others do the work, even if the goal of the campaign also benefits them. On balance, the path of least resistance is to be a free rider and not be involved.

Another element of organizer's entropy is success. As early as Saul Alinsky's first project in the Back of the Yards area of Chicago, the group that came together achieved some success and then didn't want him around anymore. If a group wins and becomes comfortable, then the motivation to do more will diminish. Organized labour faced this logic in the postwar era – having won recognition and decent contracts, its organizing dropped off. Some Canadian NGOs faced this problem in 2016 following the defeat of an unpopular prime minister who had motivated large numbers of supporters to become involved, but was now gone. ACORN finds that it needs to reorganize chapters that are falling apart, bringing in new members and shoring up leaders.

Entropy means that organizers need to keep bringing energy into the system. This energy could come from new people or new issues or both. As ACORN's Judy Duncan says, "if you are not growing, you are dying." There is an art – hard to teach – to pivoting within an issue or between issues to maintain momentum. There are more leaders who have an ability to manage a team well, but leaders who can discern pathways to victory in the face of moving obstacles are rare and should be held onto when found. Without that kind of strategic judgment somewhere in the system, entropy will take over, and people will drop out. Of course, campaigns or organizations don't have to last forever. Entropy might need to be kept at bay until the mission is fulfilled. Organizing around an election is easier, for example, since you know exactly when it's going to be over, win or lose.

Challenge: Money
Another challenge to engagement organizing is money. In theory, the good thing about the marriage of community organizing and digital tools is that it's the marriage of volunteer labour with the Internet, which is free, right? Although making connections among potential volunteer supporters is easier and cheaper than ever before, shaping and sustaining those connections takes real and consistent investments of time. The perfect snowflake with a few staff in the middle and endless tiers of volunteers radiating outward exists only in campaign mythology. The reality is that campaigns need paid organizers to constantly recruit, train, and coach others and to troubleshoot problems. They even need to "fire" volunteers who are not working out, or to avoid what Zack Exley calls the "tyranny of the annoying," whereby one disruptive volunteer can poison the well for all volunteers.

Good digital practices come with costs. Social media, free digital tools, and open source applications can get you into the game, but as a campaign scales up or wants to do specific things it will need to pay for services. And at some point somebody who knows what he or she is doing will need to be brought in to coordinate digital practices and ensure that online communications are as good as they can be. This somebody can grow to somebodies. Then there is a digital department performing core functions that need to be paid for, and odds are that the people in that department could find jobs elsewhere with bigger salaries, so they need to be compensated at a respectable level to retain them.

In sum, good engagement organizing at scale costs money. The first source of this money is the supporter base itself. This is hard-wired into labour organizing through dues, though as we've seen how much actual organizing labour dues pay for varies widely across unions. Community organizing borrowed from labour to establish a dues-based system, even when organizing in low-income communities. But the reality of ACORN and the Metro Vancouver Alliance, two of Canada's most successful community organizing examples, is that neither is self-sufficient with dues alone, and both hustle to meet their budgets. Organizations with large digital lists can tap them for donations, and for purely online groups with low overhead this can cover most, if not all, of their budgets. If those groups want to build power through organizing, though, the revenue might not be enough to cover salaries for organizers. Some groups, such as the Dogwood Initiative, therefore step up their fundraising from digital lists by switching to the phone, calling up supporters for monthly or one-time donations. It's possible to find the resources for organizing, but it's not easy.

Trend: The Fully Public Individual

The science fiction book *Accelerando* was published in 2005 by an ex-computer programmer caught up in the crazed pace of change of the dot com bubble who asked himself this question: "What happens if this goes on?" The result is his fictional world of artificial intelligence, biotechnical beings, and molecular nanotechnology. In this world, elections take place automatically based upon patterns of people's political biases expressed in communication networks. The patterns are used to "create a parliament – a merged group mind borganism that speaks as one supermind built from the beliefs of the victors."[2] There is no need for voting anymore.

Borganisms aside, the more our lives move online, the more data there are about us in the public or semi-public domain. Mass communications had the advantage of relative anonymity and privacy. One could hide in the general public or in a large demographic group. The digital era has made possible individually tailored communications, and the more people participate the more personal data are available to anyone who pays to get them. Not only is individual privacy slipping away society-wide, but also we give it away willingly with every retail loyalty card we sign up for, which aren't about loyalty at all but about collecting data. Social media companies provide us with the free service of letting us connect with friends around the world, but the actual price is that they sell the resulting patterns to those who want to reach people with qualities similar to ours. As more devices such as household appliances get connected in "the Internet of Things," data streams are generated on an increasing number of our activities.

The result is a world of ever more intimate data on every person. Where there was once a public sphere and a private sphere, there will soon be only a public sphere and a semi-public sphere available to those who pay for access to it. Unless a person lives off the grid, she or he will be a public individual. Those who value privacy are rightly alarmed by this trend. The science fiction campaign of near-perfect data on everyone involved isn't that far away. Whether the public continues to tolerate the erosion of the private sphere remains to be seen. In the meantime, campaigns have the ever-growing opportunity to connect with people who share their values and goals, with the knowledge that, if they don't use these data, then their competitors might. As campaigns navigate the loss of the private sphere and the emergence of the fully public individual, they should actively wrestle with data ethics. Supporters should have as much information about the campaign and those who run it as the campaign has about them. Transparency is perhaps the most effective way forward now that the data genie is out of the bottle and unlikely to return.

Trend: Organizing Movements

Organizing movements is the holy grail of campaigns. Shaping a genuine uprising into a major win is incredibly difficult and rare. Can we become better at it? Brothers Mark and Paul Engler study the history of social change and promote the idea of "momentum-driven organizing."[3] They draw a distinction between mass protest and structure-based organizing practised by Alinsky-inspired groups and unions and argue that they use different logics that some see as irreconcilable. Structure-based groups focus on transactional goals and by achieving them build power more slowly over time within structures or organizations. Mass protest focuses on transformational goals and burns brightly for a time to change public opinion and to set the stage for bigger policy shifts later. In this way, Occupy flamed out quickly but shifted the public debate about inequality and helped to create the conditions for politicians such as Obama and Trudeau to pursue policy solutions.

The question is whether such movement moments are entirely unpredictable and arbitrary in terms of how they unfold or whether it's possible to help create and shepherd them. The Englers think that it is possible and put forward the intriguing idea of a hybrid between structure and mass protest. A modern example is Otpor, the group that helped to topple Slobodan Milosovic in Serbia through a variety of movement-building tactics. It used a decentralized structure of independent chapters but did two things to hold it together. First, it used "frontloading" to convey a set of well-defined norms and practices for people to follow. Second, to bring supporters on board quickly, it used mass training sessions that would last about ten hours over five evenings and end with trainees executing actions themselves: "Only then were they officially considered members of the movement."[4] Otpor rotated its spokespeople so that no one or two figureheads emerged, but there were nevertheless leaders.

The practices of engagement organizing as laid out in this book are broadly consistent with the Englers' momentum-based organizing, even if the latter goes further into movement strategy. The concept of the engagement cycle is designed to accommodate slower, smaller initiatives driven primarily by paid organizers or faster, larger initiatives driven by popular sentiments. The concept of the snowflake is designed to provide a mixture of structure and independence. Each campaign will strike its own balance between the two, but as the Englers note some structure is the difference between momentum-driven organizing and simple mass protest, with the former seeking to sustain itself through multiple waves of activity.[5]

The Dean, Obama, and Sanders presidential campaigns also provide fodder for a discussion of organizing movements. Like the Otpor example, they involved a simple goal around a binary yes/no transformative choice of a leader, which made it easier for supporters to come together. They were also able to quickly absorb an influx of volunteer energy in decentralized structures. The Dean and Sanders campaigns in particular let supporters choose their own adventures and gave them tools to support them while conveying to them what was most useful in terms of voter contact. Dean and Sanders were antidotes to the "politics as pain" principle to which many subscribe – that this stuff has to be difficult. The Obama campaigns were more directive in encouraging supporters to do what was needed but still trusted them with large amounts of agency.

The Englers identify a key barrier to organizing movements: risk. Since movements are about transformational change, they fundamentally challenge vested societal interests and as such are controversial. Existing organizations often have a range of established relationships with decision makers, contracts, or accumulated assets that they don't want to risk. This makes them conservative and unwilling or unable to ride along with grassroots energy when it emerges. As such, movement moments might continue to arise with newly created organizational forms each time.

Getting Started: The Stop-Doing List

In books like this, it is often assumed that we are starting from scratch, but odds are that if you have read this far, then you are already engaged in this kind of work and have a full plate. My experience working with groups that want to move toward engagement organizing is that they first need to make room for it, to free up some bandwidth and resources. A first step might therefore be to create a "stop-doing" list. I first encountered this concept in a book about management that is also a great book for campaigners.[6] Most of us are already too busy, and the answer isn't to become busier still, so some things need to go to free up time and resources, and we need to be courageous in making those cuts.

What should be on your stop-doing list? It should begin with your campaign's or organization's theory of change, both your roadmap and your filter of what belongs and what doesn't. The ideal is to have a clear theory of change derived in a participatory manner that puts engagement organizing at its core and about which everyone in the campaign or organization is excited. If there is significant dissent about the theory of change, then there might be some tough but necessary conversations about some people finding alternative places to plug in. Without enthusiasm, there will not be success.

With a theory of change in hand, your team can begin to evaluate the major programs or activities on its plate to decide what to keep and what to cut. Questions like the following can help:

- Is this program or activity area about engaging people at scale?
- Is this program or activity area identifying, cultivating, and training leaders to help own the mission?
- Is this program or activity area integrating digital tools and practices to scale and to be nimbler?
- Is this program or activity area using data and a culture of evaluation and adaption to become more effective?
- Is this program or activity area intentional about using an engagement cycle from issue alignment to mobilization to distributed leadership and then around again?
- Is this program or activity area structuring interdependent leadership in a model like a snowflake?
- Is this program or activity area using decision making that is inclusive of all key campaign participants and accountable to all supporters?

If no is the answer to a number of questions, then a program or activity might need to be cut entirely as simply inconsistent with engagement organizing. Some inconsistent programs or activities might nonetheless be essential to your mission, but have the courage to ask if that's really true. If not, then drop them to free up resources for something else. If no is the answer to just a few questions, then a program or activity can be modified. Sometimes this might require organization-wide change, though, as in the case of needing tech systems upgrades or governance changes.

When space and resources are freed up, a more exciting conversation about new things can begin (though I have also witnessed excitement during the stop-doing list phase when unpopular commitments get axed). Which things can you do to engage your supporters more deeply and to find new ones or help them to find you? Which investments can you make in new organizers and new systems that scale up supporter involvement? How can you open up your campaign or organization to more participatory decision making by a larger leadership group? How can you increase your power? How can you win more?

Recap

Engagement organizing combines community organizing practices, digital tools, data, and networked communications to engage people at scale and win campaigns. The previous chapters explored each element in detail and provided recommendations to campaigns and organizations to implement. Here is a summary of those recommendations.

For Everyone

- *Develop an organizing-based theory of change about people acting collectively.* In all organizing, power is built by the quantity and depth of relationships aligned around a mission and the resources that those relationships can bring to bear.

- *Listen for common cause.* Organizing starts with questions, not answers. As Alinsky said, "you organize with your ears, not your mouth." Which issues do your people have in common?

- *Cultivate and train leaders to work with others to carry the mission.* Organizers do not do things for people but with them. Identify leaders and cultivate them by giving them responsibility. Use training and mentoring to develop skills and to build common cause.

- *Structure teams and accountability.* People perform best in teams connected by a common theory of change. For decision making, organizers need to be accountable to leaders, and leaders need to be accountable to one another and to other supporters.

- *Pick power-building goals, evaluate, and repeat.* Put issues through a power analysis before acting. Learn from successes and failures through reflection and evaluation. Then do it again to keep building.

- *Use digital tools to help define and engage your constituency.* You can now define a bigger community of interest, reach people more easily to help form them into a constituency, and encourage them to interact with the campaign in various ways.

- *Be nimble around faster issue cycles.* Information is now travelling more quickly, and if you aren't responding to the latest relevant news somebody else is. Decide whether that matters to your campaign.

- *Support relationships with elegant data management.* New systems let you keep all your relationship information in one place. This is your campaign brain – think clearly.

- *Measure, test, and adapt.* Why be good when you could be great? Adopt a culture of asking what works best. Measure campaign tactics and test alternatives. Make changes based upon the results.

- *Recognize the limitations of digital tools and build other power.* Campaigns aren't won online. Use digital tools to create opportunities to build solidarity in person. Build alliances with groups that bring different kinds of leverage to the table.

- *Plan for an engagement cycle.* Engagement organizing goes through overlapping phases of issue (re)alignment, mobilization, and distributed leadership. Repeating the cycle can grow the campaign or organization.

- *Align and realign issues.* Be open to grassroots energy and facilitate alignment or realignment of a critical mass of people around issues to move to action.

- *Mobilize.* Help to design higher-effort activities to advance the issue within a shared theory of change, and help to identify leaders along the way.

- *Distribute leadership.* Consider a snowflake structure to form interlocking teams of organizers, leaders, and volunteers who hold one another accountable for meeting campaign goals.

- *Network communications.* Shift from "speaking at" supporters to "speaking with" them, and foster their ability to own and carry campaign communications across their own networks – "speaking between." Meanwhile, work with both traditional and digital media outlets in the hybrid media environment.

For NGOs

- *Be aware of how the NGO sector is facing disruption and adapt.* A new generation of nimble, digital-first NGOs is emerging to compete for relevance and support. Organizations that want to thrive today must understand how to be like them.

- *Uncover sources of group inertia and overcome them.* Your staff, your systems, your organizational culture, and your governance can all be sources of inertia preventing a shift to engagement organizing. Identify and address these sources consciously.

- *Incorporate engagement organizing into your theory of change.* Any group working with people at scale can benefit from applying engagement organizing practices. Become comfortable with the concept of building power, and embrace distributed leadership.

For Unions

- *Reclaim a broader definition of organizing.* Unions helped to invent modern organizing, but a servicing model and the grievance process took over. Labour organizing can be reclaimed as building power with workers everywhere – it's never over, even in a workplace with a contract.
- *Catch up with political parties and NGOs on the use of digital tools and data to build power.* Invest in robust systems to establish, manage, and enhance conversations with members to better mobilize and organize them.
- *Go bigger and broader in organizing in the new economy.* Bigger investments and more creativity in organizing models are needed to reach the 85 percent of workers in Canada's private sector who don't belong to a union. This will determine whether labour thrives or withers.

For Electoral Actors

- *Give more of the party over to its constituency.* Open the party to meaningful participation and engagement by those whom the party wants to earn votes from and not just party insiders.
- *Shift from mass communication to individualized communication at a massive scale.* The more personal the voter contact, the more effective it is: use data and distributed teams at scale to talk to voters.
- *Be authentic.* Broadcast-era marketing has given way to politicians being themselves, warts and all. Voters want genuine, not packaged, candidates. Campaign accordingly.

I began this book with a story of personal campaign failure, which turned out to be a gift of discovery that I have shared with you in these pages. If you have been involved with campaigns for a while, odds are you have more lessons to add, and I encourage you to take the time to capture them and put them out there for others to learn from. If you are just starting out with a campaign, it's not that I wish you failure, but odds are you'll experience it too. My advice to you is to cultivate an attitude of questioning and learning, and of failing well. That will lead to more success.

We are at an exciting moment as the broadcast era erodes in the face of a digital evolution that has changed the campaign landscape. There is an opportunity to involve supporters at larger scales, more directly, more quickly, and at lower costs to build power and to win campaigns. Some organizations and campaigns are already doing so, and often they are those increasingly commanding attention and setting the agenda. Engagement organizing provides a way to win more often in a new era.

Appendix:
Advice for Rookie (Labour) Organizers

These are the twenty postulates of "Advice for Rookie Organizers," based upon the CIO-style labour organizing of the 1930s and appearing on the bulletin boards of most offices of the branch of the SEIU known as 1199 New England.

1   Get close to the workers; stay close to the workers.
2   Tell workers it's their union and then behave that way.
3   Don't do for workers what they can do [for themselves].
4   The union is not a fee for service; it is the collective experience of workers in struggle.
5   The union's function is to assist workers in making a positive change in their lives.
6   Workers are made of clay, not glass.
7   Don't be afraid to ask workers to build their own union.
8   Don't be afraid to confront them when they don't.
9   Don't spend your time organizing workers who are already organizing themselves, go to the biggest worst.
10 The working class builds cells for its own defence; identify them and recruit their leaders.
11 Anger is there before you are – channel it, don't defuse it.
12 Channeled anger builds a fighting organization.

13 Workers know the risks; don't lie to them.
14 Every worker is showtime – communicate energy, excitement, urgency, and confidence.
15 There is enough oppression in workers' lives not to be oppressed by organizers.
16 Organizers talk too much. Most of what you say is forgotten.
17 Communicate to workers that there is no salvation beyond their own power.
18 Workers united can beat the boss. You have to believe that, and so do they.
19 Don't underestimate the workers.
20 We lose when we don't put workers into struggle.

This list appears in Jane McAlevey's book *No Shortcuts: Organizing for Power in the New Gilded Age* (New York: Oxford University Press, 2016), 90–91. It appears here by permission of Oxford University Press, USA.

Notes

Introduction

1 Sasha Issenberg, *The Victory Lab: The Secret Science of Winning Campaigns* (New York: Crown Publishers, 2012), 7.
2 Donald P. Green and Alan S. Gerber, *Get Out the Vote: How to Increase Voter Turnout* (Washington, DC: Brookings Institution Press, 2015), 9.
3 Theda Skocpol, *Diminished Democracy: From Membership to Management in American Civic Life* (Norman: University of Oklahoma University Press, 2003).
4 Ibid., 163. Skocpol attributes this expression to Marshall Ganz.

Chapter 1: Organizing Principles and Training

1 For more on ACORN, see https://www.acorncanada.org/.
2 Marshall Ganz, "Leading Change: Leadership, Social Change, and Social Movements," in *Handbook of Leadership Theory and Practice: A Harvard Business School Centennial Colloquium*, ed. Nitin Nohria and Rakesh Kurna (Boston: Harvard Business Press, 2010), 4.
3 Saul Alinsky, *Rules for Radicals: A Pragmatic Primer for Realistic Radicals* (1971; reprinted, New York: Vintage Books, 1989), 12.
4 Ibid., 51.
5 Judith Taylor, "No to Protests, Yes to Festivals: How the Creative Class Organizes in the Social Movement Society," in *Protest and Politics: The Promise of Social Movement Societies*, ed. Howard Ramos and Kathleen Rodgers (Vancouver: UBC Press, 2015), 178.
6 Ibid., 186.
7 Ibid., 189.
8 Alinsky, *Rules for Radicals*, 174.
9 Jane McAlevey, *No Shortcuts: Organizing for Power in the New Gilded Age* (New York: Oxford University Press, 2016), 37.

10 Ibid., 4.
11 Alinsky, *Rules for Radicals*, 120.
12 Ibid., 113–15.
13 Mark Engler and Paul Engler, *This Is an Uprising: How Nonviolent Revolt Is Shaping the Twenty-First Century* (New York: Nation Books, 2016), 120.
14 Becky Bond and Zack Exley, *Rules for Revolutionaries: How Big Organizing Can Change Everything* (White River Junction, VT: Chelsea Green Publishing, 2016).
15 Gabriel Thompson, *America's Social Arsonist: Fred Ross and Grassroots Organizing in the Twentieth Century* (Berkeley: University of California Press, 2016), 72.
16 Aaron Schutz and Mike Miller, eds., *People Power: The Community Organizing Tradition of Saul Alinsky* (Nashville: Vanderbilt University Press, 2015), 87.
17 Marshall Ganz, *Why David Sometimes Wins: Leadership, Organization, and Strategy in the California Farm Worker Movement* (Oxford: Oxford University Press, 2009).
18 Edward T. Chambers, with Michael A. Cowan, *Roots for Radicals: Organizing for Power, Action, and Justice* (New York: Bloomsbury, 2013), 46.
19 Mark R. Warren, *Dry Bones Rattling: Community Building to Revitalize American Democracy* (Princeton, NJ: Princeton University Press, 2001), 32.
20 Chambers and Cowan, *Roots for Radicals*, 87.
21 Frank Pierson, cited in Warren, *Dry Bones Rattling*, 192.
22 Wade Rathke, "ACORN Community Organizing Model (1973)," in Schutz and Miller, *People Power*, 285–304.
23 Warren, *Dry Bones Rattling*, 223.
24 ACORN Canada, email to the author, April 1, 2016.
25 See http://www.leadingchangenetwork.org.
26 Anna Mclean, Shea Sinnott, and Peter Gibbs, eds., "Organizing: People, Power, Change," adapted from Marshall Ganz, Leading Change Network and New Organizing Institute, 4, http://d3n8a8pro7vhmx.cloudfront.net/themes/52e6e37401925b6f9f000002/attachments/original/1423171411/Organizers_Handbook.pdf?1423171411. A newer version can be found by contacting Organize BC.
27 Ibid.
28 Ibid., 16.
29 Hahrie Han, *How Organizations Develop Activists: Civic Associations and Leadership in the 21st Century* (New York: Oxford University Press, 2014), 163.
30 For more on the MVA, see http://www.metvanalliance.org/.
31 Warren, *Dry Bones Rattling*, 221.
32 Deborah Littman, interviewed by the author, Vancouver, January 14, 2016. All quotes from this person are derived from this interview, unless otherwise indicated.
33 Judy Duncan, interviewed by the author, Toronto, March 15, 2016. All quotes from this person are derived from this interview, unless otherwise indicated.
34 John Atlas, *Seeds of Change: The Story of ACORN, America's Most Controversial Antipoverty Community Organizing Group* (Nashville: Vanderbilt University Press, 2010), 12–13.
35 Madelaine Talbot, interviewed by Mike Miller, in Schutz and Miller, *People Power*, 306.
36 Cited in Atlas, *Seeds of Change*, 21.
37 Ibid., 35.

38 For more on Organize BC, see http://www.organizebc.ca/.
39 Peter Gibbs, interviewed by the author, Victoria, April 5, 2016. All quotes from this person are derived from this interview, unless otherwise indicated.
40 Cited in Mike Miller, "Saul Alinsky and His Core Concepts," in Schutz and Miller, *People Power*, 35.

Chapter 2: Digital and Data

1   For example, IAF Executive Director Edward Chambers says that "the products of the so-called electronic revolution are instruments created by the devil to keep us powerless." Edward T. Chambers, with Michael A. Cowan, *Roots for Radicals: Organizing for Power, Action, and Justice* (New York: Bloomsbury, 2013), 109.
2   Zeynep Tufekci, "Social Movements and Governments in the Digital Age: Evaluating a Complex Landscape," *Journal of International Affairs* 68, 1 (2014): 12.
3   Jeremy Heimans and Henry Timms, "Understanding 'New Power,'" *Harvard Business Review*, December 2014, https://hbr.org/2014/12/understanding-new-power.
4   David Karpf, *The MoveOn Effect: The Unexpected Transformation of American Political Advocacy* (New York: Oxford University Press, 2012), 158.
5   See, for example, Michael Patrick Lynch, *The Internet of Us: Knowing More and Understanding Less in the Age of Big Data* (New York: Liveright Publishing, 2016).
6   Theda Skocpol, *Diminished Democracy: From Membership to Management in American Civic Life* (Norman: University of Oklahoma University Press, 2003).
7   Raphael Foshay, "Introduction: The Computational Turn and the Digital Network," in *The Digital Nexus: Identity, Agency, and Political Engagement*, ed. Raphael Foshay (Edmonton: Athabasca University Press, 2016), 6.
8   See, for example, the writings of Manuel Castells.
9   Communic@tions Management Inc., "Canada's Digital Divide(s): A Discussion Paper," August 20, 2015, http://media-cmi.com/downloads/CMI_Discussion_Paper_Digital_Divides_082015.pdf, 4.
10 Canadian Radio-Television and Telecommunications Commission (CRTC), "Communications Monitoring Report 2015: Canada's Communications System: An Overview for Citizens, Consumers, and Creators," 2015, http://www.crtc.gc.ca/eng/publications/reports/policymonitoring/2015/cmr2.htm.
11 Daniel Tencer, "Cord-Cutting in Canada Nearly Doubles Its Pace: 1/4 of Homes Now Cable-Free," *Huffington Post*, April 8, 2016, http://www.huffingtonpost.ca/2016/04/08/cord-cutting-canada-tv_n_9644652.html.
12 CRTC, "Communications Monitoring Report 2015."
13 Jeff Fraser, "Canadians 35+ Still Spend More Time on Desktop than Mobile," *MarketingMag. ca*, July 21, 2015, http://www.marketingmag.ca/media/canadians-35-still-spend-more-time-on-desktop-than-mobile-152380.
14 Danah Boyd, cited in Helen Margetts, Peter Scott, John Hale, and Taha Yasseri, *Political Turbulence: How Social Media Shape Collective Action* (Princeton, NJ: Princeton University Press, 2016), 62.
15 Chris Wells, *The Civic Organization and the Digital Networked Citizen: Communicating Engagement in a Networked Age* (New York: Oxford University Press, 2015), 44.

16 See, for example, Greg Satell, "What Can We Expect from the Next Decade of Marketing?," *Forbes*, October 21, 2013, http://www.forbes.com/sites/gregsatell/2013/10/21/what-can-we-expect-from-the-next-decade-of-marketing/.

17 Margetts et al., *Political Turbulence*, 49.

18 "Millennials Support Causes, Not Institutions, Survey Finds," *Philanthropy News Digest*, July 22, 2013, http://philanthropynewsdigest.org/news/millennials-support-causes-not-institutions-survey-finds.

19 Wells, *The Civic Organization and the Digital Networked Citizen*, 172.

20 Bruce Bimber, Andrew J. Flanagin, and Cynthia Stohl, *Collective Action in Organizations: Interaction and Engagement in an Era of Technological Change* (New York: Cambridge University Press, 2012), 5.

21 Ibid., 61.

22 Maria Bakardjieva, "Navigating the Mediapolis: Digital Media and Emerging Practices of Democratic Participation," in *The Digital Nexus: Identity, Agency, and Political Engagement*, ed. Raphael Foshay (Edmonton: Athabasca University Press, 2016), 286.

23 Bimber et al., *Collective Action in Organizations*, 184.

24 Cited in Gabriel Thompson, *America's Social Arsonist: Fred Ross and Grassroots Organizing in the Twentieth Century* (Berkeley: University of California Press, 2016), 144.

25 Maria Konnikova, "The Limits of Friendship," *New Yorker*, October 7, 2014, http://www.newyorker.com/science/maria-konnikova/social-media-affect-math-dunbar-number-friendships.

26 Edward-Isaac Dovere, "How Clinton Lost Michigan – and Blew the Election," *Politico*, December 14, 2016, http://www.politico.com/story/2016/12/michigan-hillary-clinton-trump-232547.

27 This example is based upon Trevor McKenzie-Smith, interviewed by the author, Vancouver, November 21, 2016.

28 Phil Tank, "Mayor Clark Faces Challenge to Please His Supporters," [Saskatoon] *StarPhoenix*, November 7, 2016, http://thestarphoenix.com/opinion/columnists/1107-edit-tank-col.

29 Steve Anderson, interviewed by the author, Vancouver, January 15, 2016. All quotes from this person are derived from this interview, unless otherwise indicated.

30 For more on Open Media in Canada, see https://openmedia.org/en/ca.

31 Liz McDowell, interviewed by the author, Vancouver, March 3, 2016. All quotes from this person are derived from this interview, unless otherwise indicated.

32 For more on SumOfUs, see http://sumofus.org/.

33 For more on Dogwood, see https://dogwoodinitiative.org/.

34 Matt Takach, interviewed by the author via telephone, July 29, 2016. All quotes from this person are derived from this interview, unless otherwise indicated.

35 Karl Hardin, interviewed by the author, Victoria, July 27, 2016.

36 Maggie Gilbert, interviewed by the author via telephone, August 5, 2016. All quotes from this person are derived from this interview, unless otherwise indicated.

Chapter 3: Scaling and Networked Communications

1 Gail Armitage, interviewed by the author via telephone, February 3, 2016. All quotes from this person are derived from this interview, unless otherwise indicated.

2 Jason Mogus and Tom Liacas, "Networked Change: How Progressive Campaigns Are Won in the 21st Century," *NetChange,* June 2016, http://netchange.co/report.

3 Nicole Carty, "Digital Organizing in the Digital World," *Medium.com,* June 27, 2016, https://medium.com/mobilisation-journal/digital-organizing-in-the-digital-world -8a357e13bf41#.9ewtk7x1d.

4 Hahrie Han, *How Organizations Develop Activists: Civic Associations and Leadership in the 21st Century* (New York: Oxford University Press, 2014), 8.

5 Jane McAlevey, *No Shortcuts: Organizing for Power in the New Gilded Age* (New York: Oxford University Press, 2016), 13.

6 Han, *How Organizations Develop Activists,* 16–17.

7 Cited in Aaron Wherry, "Election 2015: The Snowflake and How Democracy Works," *Maclean's,* August 27, 2015, http://www.macleans.ca/politics/election-2015-the-snowflake -and-how-democracy-works/.

8 Jolan Bailey, email to the author, July 23, 2016.

9 Andrew Chadwick, *The Hybrid Media System: Politics and Power* (Oxford: Oxford University Press, 2013).

10 Ibid., 207.

11 Mogus and Liacas, "Networked Change."

12 See http://wearethe99percent.tumblr.com/.

13 Helen Margetts, Peter Scott, John Hale, and Taha Yasseri, *Political Turbulence: How Social Media Shape Collective Action* (Princeton, NJ: Princeton University Press, 2016), 69.

14 Mark Holan, "Ice Bucket Challenge Has Raised $220 Million Worldwide," *Washington Business Journal,* December 12, 2014, http://www.bizjournals.com/washington/ news/2014/12/12/ice-bucket-challenge-has-raised-220-million.html.

15 Joe Trippi, *The Revolution Will Not Be Televised: Democracy, the Internet, and the Overthrow of Everything* (2004; reprinted, New York: HarperCollins, 2008), 58–59.

16 Daniel Kreiss, *Taking Our Country Back: The Crafting of Networked Politics from Howard Dean to Barack Obama* (Oxford: Oxford University Press, 2012), 7.

17 Trippi, *The Revolution Will Not Be Televised,* 92.

18 Kreiss, *Taking Our Country Back,* 62.

19 Ibid., 58.

20 Ibid., 59.

21 Ibid., 79.

22 Sasha Issenberg, "How Obama Used Big Data to Rally Voters, Part 1," *MIT Technology Review,* December 16, 2012, https://www.technologyreview.com/s/508836/how-obama -used-big-data-to-rally-voters-part-1/.

23 Sasha Issenberg, *The Victory Lab: The Secret Science of Winning Campaigns* (New York: Crown Publishers, 2012), 248.

24 Kreiss, *Taking Our Country Back,* 21.

25 Micah L. Sifry, *The Big Disconnect: Why the Internet Hasn't Transformed Politics (Yet)* (New York: OR Books, 2014), 67.

26 Kreiss, *Taking Our Country Back,* 22.

27 Ibid., 134.

28 Ibid., 144.

29 Ibid., 145.

30 Ibid., 149.

31 Ibid., 165.

32 Elizabeth McKenna and Hahrie Han, *Groundbreakers: How Obama's 2.2 Million Volunteers Transformed Campaigning in America* (New York: Oxford University Press, 2014), 12.

33 Marshall Ganz, "How Obama Lost His Voice, and How He Can Get It Back," *Los Angeles Times,* November 3, 2010, http://articles.latimes.com/2010/nov/03/opinion/la-oe-1103-ganz-obama-20101103.

34 McKenna and Han, *Groundbreakers,* 29.

35 Cited in ibid., 53.

36 Ibid., 66–67.

37 Cited in Zack Exley, "The New Organizers: What's Really behind Obama's Ground Game," *Huffington Post,* November 28, 2008, http://www.huffingtonpost.com/zack-exley/the-new-organizers-part-1_b_132782.html.

38 Sasha Issenberg, "A More Perfect Union," *MIT Technology Review,* December 19, 2012, https://www.technologyreview.com/s/508856/obamas-data-techniques-will-rule-future-elections/.

39 Ibid.

40 Daniel Kreiss, "Digital Campaigning," in *Handbook of Digital Politics,* ed. Stephen Coleman and Deen Freelon (Cheltenham: Edward Elgar Publishing, 2015), 123.

41 Sasha Issenberg, "Part 2: How President Obama's Campaign Used Big Data to Rally Individual Voters," *MIT Technology Review,* December 17, 2012, https://www.technologyreview.com/s/508851/how-obama-wrangled-data-to-win-his-second-term/.

42 Ibid.

43 Ibid.

44 Sifry, *The Big Disconnect,* 51.

45 Richard Stallman, "Did Hipster Tech Really Save the Obama Campaign?," *Wired Magazine,* June 4, 2103, https://www.wired.com/2013/06/did-hipster-technology-really-save-the-obama-campaign/.

46 Cited in Alexis C. Madrigal, "When the Nerds Go Marching In," *The Atlantic,* November 16, 2012, https://www.theatlantic.com/technology/archive/2012/11/when-the-nerds-go-marching-in/265325/.

47 McKenna and Han, *Groundbreakers,* 3.

48 Obama/Biden, "2012 Obama Campaign Legacy Report," 70, http://secure.assets.bostatic.com/frontend/projects/legacy/legacy-report.pdf.

49 Ibid., 21.

50 Issenberg, "A More Perfect Union."

51 Obama/Biden, "2012 Obama Campaign Legacy Report," 2.

52 Cited in Sasha Issenberg, "The Meticulously Engineered Grassroots Network behind the Bernie Sanders Revolution," *Bloomberg Politics,* February 24, 2016, https://www.bloomberg.com/politics/features/2016-02-24/behind-bernie-sanders-revolution-lies-a-meticulously-engineered-grassroots-network.

53 Cited in ibid.

54 Cited in Micah Sifry, "How the Sanders Campaign Is Reinventing the Use of Tech in Politics," *The Nation,* March 14, 2016, https://www.thenation.com/article/how-the-sanders-campaign-is-reinventing-the-use-of-tech-in-politics/.

55 Nick Corasaniti, "Bernie Sanders Campaign Showed How to Turn Viral Moments into Money," *New York Times,* June 24, 2016, https://www.nytimes.com/2016/06/25/us/politics/bernie-sanders-digital-strategy.html?_r=0.

56 Michael Grothaus, "Inside Bernie Sanders's Social Media Machine," *Fast Company,* April 11, 2016, https://www.fastcompany.com/3058681/inside-bernie-sanders-social-media-machine.

57 Cited in Sifry, "How the Sanders Campaign Is Reinventing the Use of Tech in Politics."

58 Issenberg, "The Meticulously Engineered Grassroots Network behind the Bernie Sanders Revolution."

59 Cited in ibid.

60 Ibid.

61 Cited in Grothaus, "Inside Bernie Sanders's Social Media Machine."

62 Cited in Corasaniti, "Bernie Sanders Campaign Showed How to Turn Viral Moments into Money."

63 Ibid.

64 Cited in Issenberg, "The Meticulously Engineered Grassroots Network behind the Bernie Sanders Revolution."

65 Jessica McKenzie, "Zack Exley on (Maybe) the Only Problem in the Sanders Campaign," *Civicist,* June 10, 2016, http://civichall.org/civicist/zack-exley-maybe-problem-sanders-campaign/.

66 Becky Bond, cited in Sifry, "How the Sanders Campaign Is Reinventing the Use of Tech in Politics."

67 Nancy Scola, "Inside Bernie Sanders' Vast, Virtual Ground Game," *Policito.com,* April 11, 2016, http://www.politico.com/story/2016/04/bernie-sanders-virtual-ground-game-221748.

68 Will Horter, interviewed by the author, Victoria, April 27, 2016. All quotes from this person are derived from this interview, unless otherwise indicated.

69 Celine Trojand, interviewed by the author, Victoria, January 15, 2016. All quotes from this person are derived from this interview, unless otherwise indicated.

Chapter 4: Disruption in the NGO Sector

1 See, for example, the account of the Saddleback Church in Chapter 2 of Robert Putnam and David Campbell, *American Grace: How Religion Divides and Unites Us* (New York: Simon & Schuster Paperbacks, 2010).

2 David Karpf, *The MoveOn Effect: The Unexpected Transformation of American Political Advocacy* (New York: Oxford University Press, 2012), 26.

3 Mark Rovner, "The Next Generation of Canadian Giving: The Charitable Habits of Generations Y, X, Baby Boomers, and Civics," Blackbaud Inc., commissioned by hjc New Media, September 2013, http://www.hjcnewmedia.com/nextgencanadiangiving2013/downloads/The_Next_Generation_of_Canadian_Giving_2013.pdf?_ga=1.73955922.1737266837.1439409211.

4 Graham Saul, interviewed by the author, Ottawa, May 11, 2016.

5 Celine Trojand, interviewed by the author, Victoria, January 15, 2016.

6 Dean Shepherd, interviewed by the author via telephone, May 24, 2016.

7 Zeynep Tufekci, "Social Movements and Governments in the Digital Age: Evaluating a Complex Landscape," *Journal of International Affairs* 68, 1 (2014): 13.

8 Yotam Marom, "What Really Caused the Implosion of the Occupy Movement: An Insider's View," *Alternet.org*, December 23, 2015, http://www.alternet.org/occupy-wall-street/what-really-caused-implosion-occupy-movement-insiders-view.

9 Kino-nda-niimi Collective, ed., *The Winter We Danced: Voices from the Past, the Future, and the Idle No More Movement* (Winnipeg: ARP Books, 2014).

10 Gerald Taiaiake Alfred, "Indigenous Nationhood: Beyond Idle No More," *CommonDreams.org*, January 29, 2013, http://www.commondreams.org/views/2013/01/29/indigenous-nationhood-beyond-idle-no-more.

11 Micah L. Sifry, *The Big Disconnect: Why the Internet Hasn't Transformed Politics (Yet)* (New York: OR Books, 2014), 47.

12 Jodie Tonita, "#BlackLivesMatter: Lessons from a Leader-Ful Movement," *stproject.org*, blog, January 27, 2015, http://stproject.org/from-the-field/blacklivesmatter-lessons/.

13 Cited in Mary Green, "Oprah Winfrey's Comments about Recent Protests and Ferguson Spark Controversy," *People Magazine*, January 1, 2015, http://people.com/celebrity/oprah-on-recent-protests-and-ferguson/.

14 Cited in ibid.

15 Logan McIntosh, interviewed by the author, Vancouver, January 14, 2016, and via telephone, July 29, 2016. All quotes from this person are derived from these interviews, unless otherwise indicated.

16 For more on Leadnow, see http://www.leadnow.ca/.

17 Jamie Biggar, interviewed by the author, Vancouver, January 15, 2015. All quotes from this person are derived from this interview, unless otherwise indicated.

18 Leadnow, "Defeating Harper: Reflections on the Vote Together Campaign," https://s3.amazonaws.com/leadnow/vtreport/vtreport.pdf, 11.

19 Ibid., 4–5.

20 For more on Ecology Ottawa, see https://ecologyottawa.ca/.

21 Graham Saul, interviewed by the author, Ottawa, May 11, 2016. All quotes from this person are derived from this interview, unless otherwise indicated.

22 Gillian Walker, interviewed by the author, Ottawa, May 12, 2016. All quotes from this person are derived from this interview, unless otherwise indicated.

Chapter 5: Rediscovering Union Organizing

1 Statistics Canada, "Unionization Rates Falling," March 31, 2016, http://www.statcan.gc.ca/pub/11-630-x/11-630-x2015005-eng.htm.

2 Stephanie Ross, Larry Savage, Errol Black, and Jim Silver, *Building a Better World: An Introduction to the Labour Movement in Canada*, 3rd ed. (Halifax: Fernwood Publishing, 2015), 114.

3 David Camfield, *Canadian Labour in Crisis: Reinventing the Worker's Movement* (Halifax: Fernwood Publishing, 2011).

4 For example, the 2008 convention of the Canadian Labour Congress.

5 Ross et al., *Building a Better World*, 145–46.

6 Ibid., 173.

7   David Dorey, "Why Unions Can't Organize Retail Workers," *LawofWork.ca,* http://law ofwork.ca/?p=7061.

8   Canadian Labour Congress, *The Steward Handbook,* 2015, http://canadianlabour.ca/ sites/default/files/education_resource/Steward%20Handbook%20March%202015%20. pdf.

9   See, for example, Ross et al., *Building a Better World,* 122–23.

10 Camfield, *Canadian Labour in Crisis,* 43.

11 Patty Barrera, interviewed by the author, Toronto, January 25, 2016.

12 Stephanie Ross and Larry Savage, "Rethinking the Politics of Labour in Canada: An Introduction," in *Rethinking the Politics of Labour in Canada,* ed. Stephanie Ross and Larry Savage (Halifax: Fernwood Publishing, 2012), 15–16.

13 Camfield, *Canadian Labour in Crisis,* 121.

14 Jane McAlevey, *No Shortcuts: Organizing for Power in the New Gilded Age* (New York: Oxford University Press, 2016), 20.

15 Jane McAlevey, with Bob Ostertag, *Raising Expectations (and Raising Hell): My Decade Fighting for the Labour Movement* (London: Verso, 2012).

16 Ibid., 14.

17 Ibid., 299.

18 Sage Aaron, interviewed by the author, Vancouver, May 31, 2016.

19 Mark Brenner, "What If Unions Took to Heart the Need to Organize Their Own Members?," *Labor Notes,* February 24, 2015, http://www.labornotes.org/blogs/2015/02/ video-what-if-unions-took-heart-need-organize-their-own-members.

20 Sasha Issenberg, *The Victory Lab: The Secret Science of Winning Campaigns* (New York: Crown Publishers, 2012), Chapter 6.

21 Brett Caraway, "OUR Walmart: A Case Study of Connective Action," *Information, Communication, and Society* 19, 7 (2016): 907–20.

22 Pradeep Kumar, "Whither Unionism: Current State and Future Prospects of Union Renewal in Canada," IRC Research Program, Queen's University, December 2008.

23 Kendra Coulter, "Anti-Poverty Work: Unions, Poor Workers, and Collective Action in Canada," in Ross and Savage, *Rethinking the Politics of Labour in Canada,* 161.

24 Justice for Janitors, SEIU Local 2, "Toronto-Area Janitors Ratify New Deal," May 16, 2016, http://justiceforjanitors.ca/2016/05/16/a-step-forward-for-working-families-as-toronto -area-janitors-ratify-new-deal/.

25 For more information, visit http://www.workingamerica.org/.

26 Lis Pimentel, interviewed by the author, Toronto, May 10, 2016. All quotes from this person are derived from this interview, unless otherwise indicated.

27 For more on UNITE HERE Local 75, see http://www.uniteherelocal75.org/.

28 David Sanders, interviewed by the author, Toronto, May 9, 2016. All quotes from this person are derived from this interview, unless otherwise indicated.

29 Julius Getman, *Restoring the Power of the Unions: It Takes a Movement* (New Haven, CT: Yale University Press, 2010), 43.

30 Cited in ibid., 65.

31 Ibid., 73.

32 This section and the quotations are drawn from Paul Finch and Jacob Hunter, BCGEU, presentation at the CanRoots conference in Vancouver, April 23, 2016. For more on the BCGEU, see http://www.bcgeu.ca/.

Chapter 6: Electoral Organizing

1 Colin Horgan, "What Is the Point of a Political Party?," *Medium.com,* April 7, 2016, https://medium.com/@cfhorgan/what-is-the-point-of-a-political-party-6276769347a7#.w4x9qks93.

2 Stephen Clarkson, *The Big Red Machine: How the Liberal Party Dominates Canadian Politics* (Vancouver: UBC Press, 2005), 7.

3 This is the thesis running through Susan Delacourt's book *Shopping for Votes: How Politicians Choose Us and We Choose Them,* 2nd ed. (Madeira Park, BC: Douglas and McIntyre, 2016).

4 Donald P. Green and Alan S. Gerber, *Get Out the Vote: How to Increase Voter Turnout* (Washington, DC: Brookings Institution Press, 2015), 9.

5 Cited in Joan Bryden, "Trudeau Promotes Wide-Open Liberal Party, No More Membership Privileges," *Canadian Press,* April 3, 2016, http://www.macleans.ca/news/canada/trudeau-promotes-wide-open-liberal-party-no-more-membership-privileges/.

6 Clarkson, *The Big Red Machine,* 21–27.

7 Susan Delacourt, "How Policy Is Being Made under the New Liberal Government," *Policy Options,* April 26, 2016, http://policyoptions.irpp.org/magazines/april-2016/how-policy-is-being-made-under-the-new-liberal-government/.

8 Tom Parkin, "It's Raining Lobbyists in Ottawa," *Postmedia Network,* July 17, 2016, http://www.torontosun.com/2016/07/17/its-raining-lobbyists-in-ottawa.

9 Colin Bennett, "They're Spying on You: How Party Databases Put Your Privacy at Risk," *iPolitics.ca,* September 1, 2015, http://ipolitics.ca/2015/09/01/theyre-spying-on-you-how-party-databases-put-your-privacy-at-risk/.

10 Giles Tremlet, "The Podemos Revolution: How a Small Group of Radical Academics Changed European Politics," *The Guardian,* March 31, 2015, https://www.theguardian.com/world/2015/mar/31/podemos-revolution-radical-academics-changed-european-politics.

11 Pablo Iglesias, "Understanding Podemos," *New Left Review* (May–June 2015), 12.

12 Ibid., 15.

13 Tremlet, "The Podemos Revolution."

14 Iglesias, "Understanding Podemos," 19.

15 Marshall Ganz, quoted in John Judis, "Can the Democrats Get Organized: An Interview with Marshall Ganz," *Talking Points Memo,* February 24, 2017, http://talkingpointsmemo.com/cafe/can-the-democrats-get-organized.

16 Chima Nkemdirim, interviewed by the author via telephone, June 28, 2016. All quotes from this person are derived from this interview, unless otherwise indicated.

17 Marc Power, "The Nenshi Phenomenon – 2010 Election," blog, January 24, 2015, http://www.mypoliticalconsultant.com/analysis/nenshi-phenomenon-2010-election/.

18 Brian Singh, interviewed by the author via Skype, June 2, 2016.

19 Richard Einarson, interviewed by the author, Calgary, June 1, 2016. All quotes from this person are derived from this interview, unless otherwise indicated.

20 Cited in Chris Turner, "Cowtown No More: Why Calgary Chose Naheed Nenshi," *Globe and Mail,* October 22, 2010, http://www.theglobeandmail.com/news/national/cowtown -no-more-why-calgary-chose-naheed-nenshi/article565092/?page=all.

21 Ibid.

22 Chris Koentges, "Politics in Full Sentences: The Story of Naheed Nenshi's Purple Army," *Very Ethnic,* October 18, 2011, https://veryethnic.com/2011/10/18/politics-in-full -sentences-a-detailed-story-of-naheed-nenshis-purple-army/.

23 Marcello Di Cintio, "Politics 2.0 – Naheed Nenshi and the Power of Social Engagement," *Readers Digest Canada,* n.d., http://www.readersdigest.ca/features/heart/politics-20 -naheed-nenshi-and-power-social-engagement/.

24 Cited in Jessica Smith Cross, "How to Come from Behind and Win a Mayoral Campaign," *Metro News,* May 1, 2014, http://www.metronews.ca/news/toronto/2014/05/01/how-to -come-from-behind-and-win-a-mayoral-campaign-nenshi-style.html.

25 Cited in Kate Torgovnick May, "How the Mayor of Calgary Decided to Run for Office. Hint: It All Started with a TEDx Talk," *TEDBlog,* May 29, 2014, http://blog.ted.com/ mayor-of-calgary-naheed-nenshi-ran-for-office-after-giving-tedx-talk/.

26 Di Cintio, "Politics 2.0."

27 Cited in Turner, "Cowtown No More."

28 Cited in Delacourt, *Shopping for Votes,* 324.

29 Althia Raj, "Justin Trudeau's Liberals: 'We Had a Plan and We Stuck to It.' And They Won," *Huffington Post,* October 25, 2015, http://www.huffingtonpost.ca/2015/10/25/ justin-trudeau_n_8382304.html.

30 Cited in Alex Boutilier, "Liberals Outline New-Found Digital Muscle," *Toronto Star,* May 28, 2016, https://www.thestar.com/news/canada/2016/05/28/liberals-outline-new -found-digital-muscle.html.

31 Details on the Liberal field campaign were provided by an anonymous party member, interviewed by the author, Ottawa, May 12, 2016.

32 Joan Bryden, "How Old-School Volunteer Armies Use Data Analytics to Focus Campaign Efforts," *Globe and Mail,* May 31, 2015, http://www.theglobeandmail.com/news/ national/how-old-school-volunteer-armies-use-data-analytics-to-focus-campaign -efforts/article24716373/.

33 Susan Delacourt, "The Architect of a Liberal Campaign Shakeup," *Toronto Star,* September 22, 2015, https://www.thestar.com/news/federal-election/2015/09/22/the-architect-of -a-liberal-campaign-shakeup.html.

34 James Pratt, interviewed by the author, Ottawa, January 28, 2016.

35 Adam Radwanski, "Game On: Each Party's Final Push to Get Voters to the Polls," *Globe and Mail,* October 17, 2015, http://www.theglobeandmail.com/news/politics/game-on -each-partys-final-push-to-get-voters-to-thepolls/article26843129/.

36 Jennifer Hollett, interviewed by the author, Toronto, May 9, 2016.

37 Adam Radwanski, "How Data Are Giving Parties More Control over Local Campaigns," *Globe and Mail,* February 2, 2015, http://www.theglobeandmail.com/news/politics/ how-technology-is-allowing-parties-greater-control-over-local-campaigns/article 22755848/.

38 Radwanski, "Game On."

39 Bryden, "How Old-School Volunteer Armies Use Data Analytics to Focus Campaign Efforts."

40 Ibid.

41 Cited in ibid.

42 Dan Pollock, interviewed by the author, Victoria, May 5, 2016. All quotes from this person are derived from this interview, unless otherwise indicated.

43 Paul Wells, "The Winner Takes It All," *Maclean's*, November 2, 2015, 39.

44 Cited in Raj, "Justin Trudeau's Liberals."

45 Ibid.

46 Joan Bryden, "Digital Advertising Key as Liberals Outspent Tories in 2015 Vote: Elections Canada Reports," *Toronto Star*, June 20, 2016, https://www.thestar.com/news/canada/2016/06/20/digital-advertising-key-as-liberals-outspent-tories-in-2015-vote-elections-canada-reports.html.

47 Cited in Althia Raj, "Liberals Outspent Tories in Last Election, Trudeau's Adviser Gerald Butts Says," *Huffington Post*, June 15, 2016, http://www.huffingtonpost.ca/2016/06/15/liberals-spending-election-gerald-butts-trudeau_n_10476586.html.

48 Cited in Boutilier, "Liberals Outline New-Found Digital Muscle."

49 Susan Delacourt, "Liberals Outspent Tories in 2015 Campaign – and Spent Wisely," *Toronto Star*, June 17, 2016, https://www.thestar.com/news/insight/2016/06/17/liberals-outspent-tories-in-2015-campaign-and-spent-wisely-delacourt.html.

50 Campbell Clark, "After 'a Seismic Shift' in Voting, It's Time to Fill in the Political Trenches," *Globe and Mail*, June 15, 2016, http://www.theglobeandmail.com/news/politics/after-a-seismic-shift-in-voting-its-time-to-fill-in-the-political-trenches/article30483382/.

51 New Democratic Party of Canada, "Campaign 2015 Review: Working Group Report," 7, http://xfer.ndp.ca/2016/-Debrief-Report/Campaign2015Review-Report-EN-Final.pdf.

52 Michael Roy, presentation at CanRoots conference, Vancouver, April 23, 2015.

53 Raj, "Justin Trudeau's Liberals."

54 Cited in ibid.

55 Clark, "After 'a Seismic Shift' in Voting, It's Time to Fill in the Political Trenches."

56 New Democratic Party of Canada, "Campaign 2015 Review: Working Group Report."

57 David Karpf, *The MoveOn Effect: The Unexpected Transformation of American Political Advocacy* (New York: Oxford University Press, 2012), 138. Karpf draws the phrase "storming the castle" from Jon Henke, cited at 125.

58 Cited in Raj, "Liberals Outspent Tories in Last Election, Trudeau's Adviser Gerald Butts Says."

Conclusion

1 Cited by Srdja Popovic, with Matthew Millar, *Blueprint for Revolution: How to Use Rice Pudding, Lego Men, and Other Nonviolent Techniques to Galvanize Communities, Overthrow Dictators, or Simply Change the World* (New York: Spiegel and Grau, 2015), 45.

2 Charles Stross, *Accelerando*, 2005, online Creative Commons edition, http://www.antipope.org/charlie/blog-static/fiction/accelerando/accelerando-intro.html, Chapter 8.

3 Mark Engler and Paul Engler, *This Is an Uprising: How Nonviolent Revolt Is Shaping the Twenty-First Century* (New York: Nation Books, 2016).

4 Ibid., 76.
5 Ibid., 162.
6 James Collins, *Good to Great: Why Some Companies Make the Leap ... and Others Don't* (New York: HarperBusiness, 2001).

Further Resources

There are many worthwhile resources in the endnotes to this book as well as online, but here are some of the key recent books and reports for those interested in going deeper.

Bond, Becky, and Zack Exley. *Rules for Revolutionaries: How Big Organizing Can Change Everything*. White River Junction, VT: Chelsea Green Publishing, 2016.

Camfield, David. *Canadian Labour in Crisis: Reinventing the Workers' Movement*. Black Point, NS: Fernwood Publishing, 2011.

Engler, Mark, and Paul Engler. *This Is an Uprising: How Nonviolent Revolt Is Shaping the Twenty-First Century*. New York: Nation Books, 2016.

Ganz, Marshall. *Why David Sometimes Wins: Leadership, Organization, and Strategy in the California Farm Worker Movement*. New York: Oxford University Press, 2009.

Green, Donald, and Alan Gerber. *Get Out the Vote: How to Increase Voter Turnout*. 3rd ed. Washington, DC: Brookings Institution, 2015.

Han, Hahrie. *How Organizations Develop Activists: Civic Associations and Leadership in the 21st Century*. New York: Oxford University Press, 2014.

Issenberg, Sasha. *The Victory Lab: The Secret Science of Winning Campaigns*. New York: Crown Publishers, 2012.

Karpf, David. *The MoveOn Effect: The Unexpected Transformation of American Political Advocacy*. New York: Oxford University Press, 2012.

Kreiss, Daniel. *Taking Our Country Back: The Crafting of Networked Politics from Howard Dean to Barack Obama*. New York: Oxford University Press, 2012.

Margetts, Helen, Peter John, Scott Hale, and Taha Yasseri. *Political Turbulence: How Social Media Shape Collective Action*. Princeton, NJ: Princeton University Press, 2016.

McAlevey, Jane. *No Shortcuts: Organizing for Power in the New Gilded Age*. New York: Oxford University Press, 2016.

McAlevey, Jane, with Bob Ostertag. *Raising Expectations (and Raising Hell): My Decade Fighting for the Labor Movement.* London: Verso, 2012.

McKenna, Elizabeth, and Hahrie Han. *Groundbreakers: How Obama's 2.2 Million Volunteers Transformed Campaigning in America.* New York: Oxford University Press, 2014.

Mogus, Jason, and Tom Liacas. "Networked Change: How Progressive Campaigns Are Won in the 21st Century." *NetChange,* June 2016, available at netchange.co.

Skocpol, Theda. *Diminished Democracy: From Membership to Management in American Civic Life.* Norman: University of Oklahoma University Press, 2003.

Szabo, Julie, and Darren Barefoot. "Beyond the First Click: How Today's Volunteers Build Power for Movements and NGOs." *Mob Lab,* December 2016, https://mobilisation lab.org/resources/beyond-the-first-click-how-volunteers-build-power/.

Wells, Chris. *The Civic Organization and the Digital Citizen: Communicating Engagement in a Networked Age.* New York: Oxford University Press, 2015.

Index

theory of change concept, 57, *57f*, 59–61, *60f*, 80–81, 91, 155; union organizing, 108. *See also* distributed leadership; mobilization; pyramid of engagement; snowflake leadership model

Dashboard, 72
database software, 40
data management: Big Data, 42, 74; data legacy challenges, 119; data modelling, 42; digital tools, 32, 39, 40–43, 48, 54, 154; Narwhal, 72; political parties, 127; union organizing, 106, 110, 116, 119–21; voter behaviour scores, 69
days of action, 94, 139
Dean campaign, x, 6, 65–69, 73, 125, 127–29, 150–51
"DeanSpace," 67, 69
decision-making authority/governance, 61, 88, 99, 102, 109–10, 152
Democracy for America, 68
Democratic Party (US), 6, 40, 68, 130. *See also* electoral organizing
digital evolution, 31–54; campaign implications, 36–39, 50, 53–54, 61–64, 141; case studies, 43–53; data, measurement, and testing, 39–43, 127, 152; data streams, 149; lessons for engagement organizing, 53–54; old and new realities, 32–36, 121; online coalitions, 44–46; online fundraising, 74, 86, 93, 141, 148; organizing systems, 49–53, 121, 122; participatory networks, 33–34; power/power relations, 33–35; privacy issues, 43, 44, 46, 127, 149; providing surge capacity, 47–49; relationship with information, 34–36, 39, 53, 54, 61, 125. *See also* Internet/ Internet freedom; SumOfUs
digital tools: basic functions, 41–43; Bernie Dialer, 75; community organizing, 38–39, 54, 147–48, 153; data management, 40–43, 54; Dogwood's "tech stack," *52f*; engagement organ-

izing, 6–9; ethical issues, 42–43, 149; hashtags, 38; Liberal Party's "Console" analytics dashboard, 139; limitations, 53–54, 154; NDP, 139–40; NGO sector, 86, 90; political parties and campaigns, 62–63, 73–74, 125, 129–30, 136–37, 138, 141; union organizing, 119–21, 122
direct mail, 6, 85, 86, 87
distributed leadership: campaigns, 61, 79, 94, 145; concept, ix-x, 9; electoral organizing, 77, 143; engagement cycle, 57–59, *57f*, *60f*, 83, 152, 154, 155; Ganz framework, 20–21, 27, 80, 101; movement organizing, 91–92, 99; NGO sector, 89–90, 102; union organizing, 108. *See also* snowflake leadership model
Dogwood Initiative, x, 29, 49–53, 55, 77–82, 85, 86, 148

Ecology Ottawa, 85, 97–101
1199 New England (labour organizing advice), 157–58
election laws, 126–27
electoral organizing, 123–44; "air war"/"ground game," x; authenticity, 35–36, 129–30, 132, 140, 144, 155; campaign logic, 131–32; case studies, 130–43; coffee parties, 133, 134; election finance system, 126–27; election laws, 127; individualized communications, 9, 125, 144, 149, 155; issue alignment, 79, 81–83; lessons for engagement organizing, 143–44, 155–56; Liberal Party, 96–97, 123–24, 126–27, 136–43, *142f*; as movements, 125–29, 143; New Democratic Party (NDP), xiii, 97, 136–43, 137–38, *142f*; Operation Purple Dawn campaign, 129, 130–36; party ownership, 124–30, 144, 155; populism, 121, 127, 129–30; theory of change concept, 95–96, 97, 129–30, 139; 2015 Canadian election, 94–97, 136–43; voter turnout, 143.

whole worker organizing, 109. *See also* campaigns/campaign strategy

Otpor (Serbia), 150

Ottawa, Ecology Ottawa, 97–101

Oxfam, 98

patronage, 124, 125

payday lending practices, 27

peer coaching networks, 29

philanthropy/charitable giving, x–xi. *See also* foundations

phoning/phone banks, 5, 42, 52, 69, 73, 75, 81–82

Plone, 49, 50, 51

Podemos movement (Spain), 127–29

political campaigns: authenticity, 35–36, 129–30, 132, 140, 144, 155; candidate authenticity, 35–36, 129–30, 132, 140, 144, 155; central components, 75; digital tools, 125; goal setting, 150–51; political advertising, 124–25, 168n3; transactional campaigns, 77. *See also* campaigns/campaign strategy; electoral organizing

political parties: accountability, 125; broadcast era, 61–64, 124–25; clientistic model, 124; data management, 127; days of action, 94, 139; digital tools, 125, 129–30, 136; impact of Internet, 32, 33, 66, 125; individualized communications, 9, 125, 144, 149, 155; leadership, 124–25; local campaigns, 125, 139; membership, 36, 125–26, 136–37; as movements, 125–29, 136, 143; ownership of, 124–30; party structure, 126–27; restructuring, 136–37; supporter category, 136. *See also* campaigns/campaign strategy; electoral organizing; theory of change concept

populism, 121, 127, 129–30

Populous database, 138

power/power relationships: agency and empowerment, xi, 34, 82, 89–92; digital tools, 33–35; forms of, 14–15;

leadership issues, 90–92; power-building goals, 30, 153; power mapping, 16, 21; vested interests, 89

privacy concerns, 43, 44, 46, 127, 149

Putnam, Robert, 24

pyramid of engagement, 45–46, 56, 57, 90, 99. *See also* cycle of engagement; ladder of engagement

rapid response organizations/strategy, 46, 47, 49, 94, 97

Rathke, Wade, 25, 26

recruitment: ACORN Canada, 26; Camp Obama, 71; Democracy for America, 68; electoral campaigns, 70–71, 74, 95–96, 125, 131–32, 137, 139; engagement organizing, 4, 6; leaders, 16, 22, 157; methods, 17, 25–26, 28, 50, 80, 100, 110, 115, 125; Organize BC, 28–29; union organizing, 102, 110, 111–12, 115, 155; volunteers, 137–40, 143, 147, 150. *See also* mobilization

Reforest London (Ontario), 89–90

Regeneration house parties, 93, 95

religious institutions, 18, 23–24

rights-based groups, 5–6

Ross, Fred, 17

Salesforce, 40, 49, 52

Sanders, Bernie, campaign, 65, 73–76, 127, 129, 150–51

segmentation, 41–43, 50, 53, 56, 71

SEIU (Service Employees International Union), 111

September 11, 2001, xii

service model, 10, 16, 27–30, 104–7, 109–10

Sirabella, Vincent, 113–14

Skocpol, Theda, 5, 34

Slack (online collaboration app), 75, 76

smartphones, 32, 34, 35

snowflake leadership model: concept, x, 9, 21, 56–61, *57f, 60f*, 64, 83; Dogwood Initiative, 80–81; Ecology Ottawa, 99, 101; electoral organizing, 70–73, 94,

27–30, 104–7, 109–10; strikes, 108–9;
union stewards, 119–21; whole worker
organizing, 109. *See also* cycle of
engagement
United Farm Workers, 17–18, 68
United Food and Commercial Workers
(UFCW), 110–11
United Steelworkers Canada, 110
UNITE HERE local 75, 113–18, 146
US presidential campaigns, 4, 40, 65–77,
125, 127. *See also* Clinton, Hillary,
campaigns; Dean campaign; electoral
organizing; Obama campaigns;
Sanders, Bernie, campaign; Trump
campaign

vanity metrics, 48
Victory Lab (Issenberg), 4
virtual ID, 69
Vision Vancouver, 119
volunteer campaign activity: ACORN
Canada, 25–27; Canadian 2015
election, 136–43; Clark mayoral
campaign (Saskatoon), 42; Dean campaign, 6, 66–68, 124–25, 127, 150;
Dogwood Initiative, 50–51, 79–80,
82; Ecology Ottawa, 98–99; Leadnow
campaign, 95–97; Obama campaigns,
6, 51, 69–73, 71, 125, 127, 130, 137,
150; Operation Purple Dawn, 130–36;
Organize BC, 28–30; Sanders, Bernie,
campaign, 73–76, 127, 150
volunteers: agency, 59–60; coffee parties,
133, 134; days of action, 94, 139;

fieldwork/ground game, 4, 71, 73, 94,
96, 140, 143; goal setting, 150–51;
history, 5–6; ladder of engagement,
57, 74–75, 95, 120; Liberal Party, 136,
137–38; New Democratic Party (NDP),
140; online tools, 45, 98–99; organizational culture, 88; phoning/phone
banks, 5, 42, 52, 99; recruitment, 115,
137–40, 143, 147, 150; scaling, 56, 58;
segmentation, 41–42; snowflake
leadership model, 59, *60f*, 61, 83, 99,
137–38, 147, 154; union organizing,
118. *See also* campaigns/campaign
strategy; cycle of engagement
Voter Activation Network (VAN), 68
voters: autonomy, 130; behaviour scores,
69; strategic voting, 96; turnout, 143;
voter "buckets," 42; vote splitting,
95–97

Wikipedia, 33
Wilhelm, John, 114
Winter We Danced, The, 91
Women's March on Washington, xiii
WordPress, 51, 52
Workers Action Centre (Toronto), 112
Working America, 112
workplace organizing. *See* union
organizing

Yahoo!, 67
YouTube, 137

Zuccotti Park, 33

Matt Price has twenty years of experience working on campaigns of all kinds in both Canada and the United States. He has served with grassroots groups with no money and large organizations with multi-million dollar budgets. He was Campaigns Director with Environmental Defence Canada and has served as an advisor to multiple NGOs and philanthropic foundations. He has written on the subjects of campaigns and organizing in outlets like *iPolitics* and *The Huffington Post*. He lives on Vancouver Island, BC.